Title:

Untangling Knots in our Past: Navigating Unresolved Memories through Biblical Wisdom

Contents

Introduction

Have you ever felt like you would get fired at any time from your job, for no apparent reason? Have you ever felt like people were talking bad about you when they were speaking a foreign language? Or how about this one; have you ever wondered why you appear to be drawn to the "wrong" people?

These questions may resonate with many of us, as we've all experienced moments of doubt, insecurity, and self-questioning. Often, these feelings can be signs that there are knots in the lines of our memories – intricate tangles of past experiences and emotions that influence our present thoughts and actions.

These knots are significant because, if left unaddressed, they can dictate the choices we make in life. They can deter us from pursuing our dreams, hinder our personal and professional growth, and keep us trapped in a cycle of self-doubt. These knots can make us question our abilities and potential, preventing us from taking risks and embracing new opportunities. In essence, they limit our potential.

As you embark on this transformative journey, I want to share that my intention to write about this topic was not a planned endeavor. However, recent inspiration and the guidance of the Holy Spirit have led me to discover a method that can help individuals, whether they believe in God or are still searching for their faith, to access and surface their brilliance.

This book is not just about identifying the knots that may be holding you back; it's about learning how to untangle them and unleash your true potential. It's a journey of self-discovery and healing, that will enable you to break free from the limitations of your past and step into the fullness of your future.

For those who may be familiar with my first book "The Art of Surfacing Your Brilliance" this work builds upon those concepts. While the first book primarily served as a work journal, this one delves deeper into the process of unearthing your brilliance. I recommend reading it after this book, as it will provide additional insights and tools to enhance your journey.

If you've ever wondered what's been holding you back or felt the weight of unresolved memories, join me as we explore the profound impact of these knots and learn how to set ourselves free. It's time to embrace your brilliance and let it shine brightly.

Author's Background and Intentions

As a child, I spent many of my earlier days immersed in the simple joys of outdoor play, alongside my cousins. We climbed trees, ran barefoot during the summers, and engaged in spirited sandlot basketball and football games. These memories of carefree outdoor adventures serve as a stark contrast to the internal knots that later formed within me, shaping my identity and affecting my behavior.

My mother often shared stories of my infancy, recounting that I was a remarkably happy baby who woke up mostly in a great mood. It's fascinating how our demeanors and temperaments can change and evolve, reflecting the formation and untangling of the knots within our inner selves.

At the time of writing this book, I wear multiple hats in my life. I am a college professor, lead pastor of Ready 2 Serve Ministries, and a leader within a public school district. I share these facets of my life not to impress but to convey the diverse perspectives and experiences interwoven into the fabric of this book.

Having resided in the Pacific Northwest for nearly 30 years, I bring with me a blend of influences from the South, particularly the Mississippi delta region, where I originally hail from. These rich experiences have shaped my understanding of knots—both internal and external—and the profound impact they can have on our lives.

My hope for this text is that it will serve as a source of inspiration for generations to come, helping individuals navigate the complexities of their internal landscapes and providing guidance on how to untangle the knots that hinder personal growth and healing. I aspire to yield to the Holy Spirit's guidance as I organize and commit my thoughts to paper, drawing from both my personal experiences and the spiritual insights gained from supporting many individuals dealing with trauma associated with knotted up memories.

Through the pages of this book, I aim to shed light on the knots that bind us, offer strategies for understanding and addressing them, and ultimately, provide a path toward greater freedom, spiritual growth, and inner peace.

Anticipated Impact of the Text

If you are reading this book, I believe it is not by chance but by divine guidance. I pray that this book holds a Rhema, a timely and relevant message for the season of life you find yourself in. This book is a multifaceted resource encompassing themes of healing, deliverance, education, and inspiration. It aligns with the biblical encouragement to let our light shine, allowing others to see our good works. We accomplish this divine mission through sharing our testimonies and the brilliance that God has bestowed upon us.

The world hungers for your brilliance, and the consistent way we can collectively share it is by untangling the knots in our past. You will delve deeper into this concept as you progress through the book. My hope is that this resource will complement existing materials on deliverance and healing, guiding you on a path to becoming the person God has called you to be. This book is an additional offering, sharing how the Holy Spirit led me to healing and revealed how critical it was to deal with past memories in my own journey. I pray that these experiences will assist you as you pursue healing from God the father.

The origins of our internal knots—those unresolved memories and ingrained patterns of behavior—can be complex and multifaceted. While many of these knots are formed throughout our lifetime as a result of our experiences, relationships, and choices, there is compelling evidence that suggests some knots may be inherited or connected to what are termed generational curses (knots) are often connected to 'familial spirits.'

Internal knots are like intertwined threads within our psyche, representing unresolved memories, behavioral patterns, and emotional scars that have shaped our identity. These knots can often be traced back to unfavorable actions that were once congruent with who we were at the time. These actions may have resulted in people being hurt, relationships strained, and trust and confidence lost. Understanding the roots of these knots is crucial for personal growth and healing.

Many of our internal knots stem from our past actions and choices. At various points in our lives, we may have made decisions that were congruent with our circumstances and beliefs at the time but ultimately led to negative outcomes. These unfavorable actions can create knots of guilt, regret, and shame within us. For example, betraying a friend's trust, engaging in unethical behavior, or causing harm to someone can leave lasting emotional scars.

Children are particularly vulnerable to developing knots because their understanding of the world is still evolving. The world often appears simple and black-and-white to them, yet the reality is far more complex. When children are exposed to unfavorable actions or harmful experiences, their young minds may struggle to process these events. These unresolved childhood traumas can manifest as knots later in life, impacting their emotional well-being and behavior.

While the majority of our knots are formed through our own experiences, evidence suggests some knots may be inherited through what are referred to as generational curses that are connected to 'familial spirits.'

This idea suggests that certain unresolved issues or patterns of behavior within a family lineage can be passed down from one generation to the next. For instance, if a family has a history of addiction or destructive relationships, the internal knots associated with these issues may be carried forward, affecting subsequent generations.

Generational Curses and Familial Spirits: A Biblical Perspective

In the Bible, familial spirits are not explicitly described in the modern sense of generational curses or inherited spiritual problems. However, the concept is often linked to scriptures that speak of iniquities of the fathers being visited upon children and grandchildren (Exodus 20:5). This idea posits that certain negative patterns, tendencies, or "spirits" can be passed down through family lines, affecting subsequent generations. The following are two examples of this concept:

Example 1: In Exodus 20:5 (NIV), it is written, "You shall not bow down to them or worship them; for I, the Lord your God, am a jealous God, punishing the children for the sin of the parents to the third and fourth generation of those who hate me." This verse is often cited when discussing the idea of familial spirits. While it doesn't explicitly mention "familial spirits," it suggests a connection between the sins of ancestors and their impact on later generations.

Example 2: Consider a family where alcoholism has been a recurring problem. In this context, the concept of familial spirits might come into play. The idea is that the predisposition to alcoholism or the struggle with addiction is not solely a matter of personal choices but may have roots in the family's history.

This generational pattern could be seen as a form of familial spirit, affecting various family members over time. Understanding the concept of familial spirits is not necessarily about assigning blame but rather acknowledging the role of generational patterns and tendencies in shaping our internal landscape. It emphasizes the importance of breaking free from these inherited knots to lead healthier, more fulfilling lives.

Example 3: Imagine a person from a family with a history of financial hardship and irresponsible spending. Despite their best efforts, this individual finds themselves struggling with money management. The concept of familial spirits might be invoked to explain that the patterns of financial mismanagement and hardship have been passed down through generations, affecting their current situation. Breaking free from this familial spirit would involve recognizing these patterns and making conscious efforts to change them through better financial choices and education.

In summary, the concept of generational curses is rooted in biblical verses like Exodus 20:5 and is often used to explain how generational patterns and tendencies can impact individuals and families. It's a way of understanding the potential influence of past generations on our lives without necessarily assigning blame. In addition to this, our internal knots are often born from unfavorable actions congruent with who we were at the time.

They can result from our own choices, especially during vulnerable stages of life like childhood. Additionally, the idea of familial spirits suggests that some knots may have roots in generational patterns and unresolved issues. Recognizing the origins of our knots is the first step towards untangling and healing them, ultimately allowing us to grow, develop, and lead more balanced lives.

If this area has been highlighted in your spirit, I would like to recommend you look at the book 'Pigs in the Parlor,' a book on deliverance ministry by Frank and Ida Mae Hammond. This book delves into the concept of familial spirits. The Hammonds discuss how these spirits operate, affecting individuals in various areas such as emotions, will, mind, and body. They suggest that familial spirits can be responsible for recurring problems that have a history within a family, including specific sins, attitudes, and diseases.

Familial Spirits and Generational Influences

Addressing and untangling these familial knots can be different from dealing with patterns we have personally developed. According to the Hammonds and other spiritual texts, deliverance and breaking of generational curses or influences require specific spiritual intervention. The foundation for this process often lies in forgiveness, a powerful 'spiritual technology' that can disrupt the cycle of negative patterns being passed down.

As presented in the Bible, forgiveness is not just a one-time event but a profound and ongoing process that can lead to healing and freedom. Ephesians 4:31-32 encourages believers to "let all bitterness, wrath, anger, clamor, and evil speaking be put away from you, with all malice. And be kind to one another, tenderhearted, forgiving one another, even as God in Christ forgave you." This scripture underlines the importance of letting go of past hurts and choosing to forgive, which can break the hold of familial spirits.

The Role of Forgiveness in Healing

Forgiveness is a necessity; it is not merely a superficial act but a profound expression of faith and obedience to the teachings of Christ. It represents a commitment to follow the path illuminated by God's redemptive love, especially when confronted with life's most challenging trials. Forgiveness, as experienced by believers, has transformative power. It impacts one's spiritual well-being and extends its influence to physical, mental, and emotional healing.

Recognize the Meaning of Forgiveness

In certain respects, discussing what forgiveness is not makes it simpler to understand. To forgive is not to accept the other person's actions or to say that it would be acceptable for them to repeat them. It does not imply that we should ignore our own hurt sentiments or that the offending party should not face repercussions. Reconciling with the wrongdoer or forgetting that something unpleasant ever happened are not prerequisites for forgiveness.

Letting go of grudges that hold us connected to the wrongs done to us is a necessary part of forgiveness. It involves letting go of hurt, anger, or pointless ruminating so that we do not waste too much mental or emotional power on them and go on with our lives. In this sense, we should forgive ourselves just as much, if not more, than the other person or persons.

Forgiveness shines as a ray of hope and healing in the broad terrain of human emotions and moral values. We frequently see forgiveness as a virtue to be cherished, an act of love, and an order from God. But let us take a fresh look at this life-changing deed—a look at the various ways that forgiveness enhances the life of the one who is forgiving. It is a great gift that we give to ourselves as well as to others: forgiveness. This essay explores the various advantages that forgiving confers on the forgiver, transforming it into a delightful form of retaliation that surpasses bitterness.

Forgiveness is like a salve for the spirit; it gives the forgiver a deep sense of calm and inner peace. When we are filled with bitterness and wrath, our inner world seems to never end. But forgiveness has the ability to calm this storm. Peace and tranquility enter the heart via forgiveness—the releasing of the hold those harmful emotions once held over you. This inner calm is independent of the outside world; it is a calm haven that provides comfort among life's upheavals.

The Act of Forgiveness is a Doorway to Profound Healing in Multiple Dimensions of our Lives:

Physical Healing:

Carrying the weight of anger, resentment, and unforgiveness can take a toll on our physical health. Chronic stress resulting from these negative emotions can contribute to various health issues, such as high blood pressure, heart problems, and weakened immune function. Forgiveness, in contrast, liberates us from this toxic burden, potentially promoting better physical health.

The benefits of forgiveness go beyond our mental and emotional health to include our physical health. Our health may suffer as a result of ongoing hatred and rage, which are frequently linked to unforgiveness.

Physical diseases, including high blood pressure, heart difficulties, weakened immune systems, and other health disorders are caused by ongoing stress and negative emotions. On the other hand, making the decision to forgive results in reduced stress, better cardiovascular health, and increased physical vigor. It is a means of taking care of our bodies so that we might live longer, healthier lives.

Mental Healing:

Unforgiveness is a heavy load for the mind to bear, often leading to anxiety, depression, and other mental health challenges. When we choose to forgive, we free ourselves from the mental turmoil that unforgiveness brings. It is a significant step towards peace of mind and overall mental well-being.

Based on my personal encounters, being unforgiving goes beyond merely harboring resentment; it can have detrimental effects on our psychological well-being. Unforgiveness has a mental cost that can lead to despair, anxiety, and other mental health problems. It can also trigger a whirlwind of unpleasant feelings that can overtake us.

Repeating painful experiences over and over in our brains can make them feel worse, causing the wounds to get deeper and the negative cycle to continue. Having unforgiveness is like having a black cloud over our heads, preventing us from finding peace and closure and putting a strain on our mental health.

You can start to heal your emotional wounds and let go of bad feelings by forgiving others. Since it enables you to let go of any anger, resentment, or bitterness that might prevent you from moving on, forgiveness is a very effective tool in the healing process.

Refusing to forgive or harbor grudges simply serves to exacerbate your own pain and impede your own development. Studies have indicated that forgiving might benefit your physical and emotional health. Hiding away from unpleasant feelings might make you more stressed out, which can be bad for your general health. You can lower stress and foster inner calm by engaging in forgiving practices. This enhances your physical and mental health in addition to your emotional well-being.

Forgiveness is also a crucial component of the healing process. It enables you to go on with your life and let go of old hurts. Holding onto grudges or hatred toward someone who has harmed you leaves you mired in suffering and misery. Instead, you give yourself the chance to develop and transform on a personal level when you choose forgiveness.

You can let go of bad feelings and start the healing process for your emotional injuries by forgiving other people. Allowing yourself to move on from previous hurts and move on with your life is one way forgiveness fosters personal growth. You can have better general health and emotional well-being by practicing forgiveness on a regular basis.

Recall that forgiveness is about releasing oneself from the weight of holding those unfavorable feelings, not about accepting or forgetting what happened. Although the psychological cost of unforgiveness is a hefty weight that saps our spirits, we do not have to bear it alone.

We can start the process of releasing ourselves from the bonds of negativity and finding inner peace by realizing the psychological costs of unforgiveness and taking action toward forgiveness and healing.

Though it takes strength, introspection, and a readiness to let go, we may start to unravel the webs of anger and bitterness that tie us. The mental war against unforgiveness is not easily won. I am the actual evidence.

It is not forgiveness to disregard the hurt someone has caused us or to justify their behavior. It is about choosing to move forward with a lighter heart and a clearer mind, freeing us from the weight of carrying that suffering. Forgiveness is a salve for the scars from the past and a spur to development and change.

Let us have the courage to face our inner oppression, our anxieties, and our insecurities head-on, and choose the road of healing and forgiveness. It is up to us to decide. It is ours to set off on this quest. Furthermore, the benefits are enormous. Let us choose recovery and release ourselves from the eerie confines of unforgiveness.

Emotional Healing:

Emotional wounds caused by past hurts and offenses can linger, hindering our capacity to experience joy and fulfillment. Forgiveness enables us to confront these emotional wounds and find healing, leading to greater emotional resilience and a deeper sense of happiness.

In important ways, forgiveness liberates us emotionally. Having grudges is like having a lot of emotional baggage everywhere we go. It ties us up in knots of negativity. However, the secret to escaping this mental captivity and regaining the freedom to let our hearts fly is forgiveness.

While it does not take away the hurt, forgiveness allows us to move past it. It is the key that opens the door to emotional freedom, releasing us from the burden of our past wounds so that we can feel joy, happiness, and love.

Emotional scars can be healed, and the agony of the past can be released with forgiveness. By choosing to forgive, you are not downplaying or rejecting the pain you have endured. Rather, you are admitting your suffering and making the decision to let it go.

By allowing you to let go of the unfavorable feelings that are preventing you from moving forward, forgiveness makes room for development, healing, and emotional stability. The significance of forgiveness is underscored throughout the Bible, not only as a means of personal healing but also as an act of obedience to God's Word:

Matthew 6:14-15 (NIV): "For if you forgive other people when they sin against you, your heavenly Father will also forgive you. But if you do not forgive others their sins, your Father will not forgive your sins." This passage emphasizes the reciprocal nature of forgiveness—our forgiveness from God is interconnected with our willingness to forgive others.

Colossians 3:13 (NIV): "Bear with each other and forgive one another if any of you has a grievance against someone. Forgive as the Lord forgave you." Here, forgiveness is presented as an imitation of God's forgiveness of our own sins. It's an act of obedience to God's example.

Self-Forgiveness:

It's essential to note that forgiveness is not only about forgiving others but also about self-forgiveness. We often carry guilt and self-condemnation for our past mistakes. Just as we are called to forgive others, we are called to extend that same grace to ourselves as an act of obedience to God's Word.

Forgiving in faith is a transformative act that leads to physical, mental, and emotional healing. It is a profound expression of obedience to God's teachings, encompassing both forgiveness of others and self-forgiveness.

By choosing to forgive, we step into the light of God's redemptive love, trusting in His power to heal and restore, even in the darkest moments of hurt. In this journey of forgiveness, Christians affirm their faith and obedience to a higher calling, allowing God's love to bring healing and renewal to their lives.

I find self-forgiveness to be very difficult when it comes to acknowledging my wrongdoings. I have a propensity to be hard on myself, punishing and berating myself more than I would others. It feels impossible to forgive myself; it is like I am hiding or acting like someone I am not. It can be difficult to forgive oneself at times because we are afraid of repeating our mistakes.

We may believe that our negative emotions are justified. But in actuality, clinging to those emotions does not benefit us in the slightest. Understand that our inability to forgive ourselves prevents us from becoming better. Healing cannot take place when one is mired in a cycle of regret and shame!

Life can be difficult if you are carrying remorse for past actions. It can cause you to feel depressed, anxious, and unable to move on. Remaining guilty might be likened to toting a bulky rucksack filled with unfavorable emotions.

Acknowledging what you did was unacceptable is necessary, but forgiving self also entails choosing to let go of those burdensome emotions. It is akin to granting yourself permission to grow from the experience and go forward with a more accepting view of yourself.

The Complexity of Forgiveness

Acknowledging the complexity of forgiveness is essential. It's straightforward to say "forgive and forget" when the slights are small, but what about when the wounds cut deep? What of the betrayals that break hearts, the injustices that shake our sense of right and wrong, or the pain that seems too great to bear? These are the moments when forgiveness feels like an insurmountable peak.

Yet, it is precisely in these hardest of situations that forgiveness becomes a profound act of faith. To forgive in such circumstances is to trust in the "great Forgiver"—to emulate Christ, who forgave even when faced with the ultimate betrayal and suffering. It is to exercise our faith, believing that there is a purpose beyond our pain and that God's command to forgive is not without its divine reasoning. An example of this involves knots forming between God the father and us, as we attempt obey him.

Thus, scripture encourages us to 'cover ourselves with kindness, tenderness, humility, gentleness, and patience as God's chosen people, holy, and greatly loved'. Additionally, we are instructed to be patient with one another. (Colossians 3:12-13) Forgiving others as the Lord has forgiven us. This command does not reference the burden and internal struggle that may arise if we attempt to do so.

Yet we must move forward despite our weariness and emotional burdens. Often these situations are exhausting and draining, but we attempt to be strong while begrudgingly building and storing resentment.

This burden of resentment is often comprised of our past deeds, thoughts, emotions, experiences, and often distorted perceptions, all manifesting in various forms. It can appear we are condemned to carry this weight indefinitely, as it never seems to diminish. And unfortunately, as we continue our journey, more sticks may be added to our load.

Yet, while we may have imposed this burden upon ourselves or had it thrust upon us by others, we need not resign ourselves to a lifetime of carrying it. We possess the ability to unburden ourselves, one stick at a time, and alleviate the load by tapping into the spiritual resources provided by prayer. However, this process of unloading hinges on our willingness to both extend and accept forgiveness.

As our burdens lighten and the process of forgiveness takes root, our connection with God as our Father, His people as our siblings, and our familial relationships—as fathers, mothers, sisters, and brothers—will become more authentic. Sin has burdened us, but the crux of the matter lies in engaging in prayer that is efficacious, facilitating the repair of fractured relationships and fostering reconciliation following our own transgressions or those committed against us.

Through such prayer, we seek to resolve conflicts and alleviate the weight of our burdens. Effective prayer adheres to God's guidelines, granting us deeper insights into the nature of sin and its repercussions.

A few examples of this include Denise's and Al's testimonies. After undergoing hours of counseling and prayer, Denise reflected, "I never fully grasped the magnitude of the consequences, both for myself and others, resulting from my choices to sin." When we adhere to the specifications of prayer as outlined by God, we witness His response. In his journey of forgiveness, confession, and receiving forgiveness from God, Alexpressed, "I was unaware that prayer could yield tangible outcomes."

Engaging in open dialogue about our actions or the actions of others helps alleviate tension and anxiety, offering a sense of purification to some extent. However, mere conversation does not lighten our burdens. Discussing our issues helps align our thoughts with our emotions, yet it is only through God's intervention that true resolution is achieved.

Genuine forgiveness requires a divine exchange facilitated by God, allowing us to permanently shed our burdens. To attain genuine forgiveness, we must adopt God's perspective: His view of the parties involved, His understanding of the wrongdoing or sin, and His concept of forgiveness itself.

Apostle Tony Kemp, a renowned teacher and spiritual leader, offers a unique perspective on the complexity of forgiveness. He delves into a concept that may initially sound paradoxical: forgiving God. While God, in His divine nature, does not require our forgiveness, Apostle Tony Kemp emphasizes that this idea serves to highlight the intricate knots that can form between us and God.

In his teachings, Apostle Tony Kemp challenges us to consider situations where we may harbor resentment or bitterness towards God. These moments often arise when we question why certain hardships, tragedies, or injustices have befallen us or our loved ones. It's in these deeply emotional and perplexing moments that the act of forgiving God becomes relevant.

Apostle Kemp encourages us to recognize that forgiving God is not about absolving God of any wrongdoing, for God is perfect and just. Instead, it is about releasing ourselves from the burdens of anger, doubt, and confusion that can hinder our spiritual growth. It is an acknowledgment that our limited human perspective may not always fully grasp the divine plan.

In this context, forgiveness takes on a deeper meaning. It becomes a means of surrendering our need for answers and control, allowing us to trust in God's wisdom and sovereignty. It is an act of faith that goes beyond human comprehension, mirroring Christ's forgiveness on the cross, even in the face of His own suffering and betrayal.

Apostle Tony Kemp's teachings on forgiving God invite us to confront the intricate emotions and questions that can strain our relationship with him. Through this process, we may find healing, restoration, and a deeper connection with God, ultimately embracing forgiveness as a transformative act of faith on our spiritual journey.

In my view, genuine forgiveness necessitates experiencing the emotions present at the time of the offense. Rather than just the intellectual understanding of the wrongdoing, these emotions linger beneath the surface, influencing our present lives significantly and contributing greatly to the burden we carry.

Unfortunately, Western culture often discourages the expression of emotions. We are advised to remain composed, control ourselves, or remove ourselves from emotional situations. Our education system emphasizes linear thinking, prioritizing logic and reason while downplaying the significance of emotions. However, this perspective is flawed.

Our emotions are valid, and we are entitled to them. It is natural to feel pain, anger, bitterness, hurt, and humiliation when we have been wronged, or wronged others. Emotions and rational thinking are not mutually exclusive; our feelings provide context to our thoughts. Deep emotional experiences are just as valid as rational thoughts despite what we may believe.

This is why Christ emphasized the importance of internal attitudes and intentions, stating, "You have heard that it was said, 'Do not commit adultery.' But I tell you that anyone who looks at a woman lustfully has already committed adultery with her in his heart" (Matthew 5:27-28). Our thoughts and feelings hold significant weight, equivalent to tangible actions. Therefore, it is imperative that we view our own actions and the actions of others through the lens of both reason and emotion, aligning ourselves with God's perspective.

Forgiving in Faith

From a spiritual perspective, holding onto unforgiveness can have severe consequences. It weakens your spirit and renders your prayers ineffective. Unforgiveness can diminish your faith to such an extent that you lack the strength to overcome even minor challenges, let alone the major obstacles in your life.

In one of His teachings on faith, Jesus emphasized the importance of forgiveness, stating, "And when ye stand praying, forgive, if ye have aught against any..." (Mark 11:25). Jesus didn't suggest forgiveness as an option; He commanded it unequivocally.

Jesus' command to forgive implies that it is within our capacity to do so, regardless of the circumstances. Often, unforgiveness stems from fear—fear of being hurt again, fear of not being able to recover from the damage inflicted upon us by others.

Despite such fears, we can take solace in the assurance that God will provide for all our needs (Philippians 4:19). By embracing the knowledge of God's merciful and protective love, we can overcome our fears (1 John 4:18).

Forgiveness should be approached with faith, not based on fleeting emotions. It is akin to receiving healing or any other blessing through faith. First, make a firm decision to obey God's command to forgive.

Second, align your words and actions with this decision. Refrain from speaking negatively about those who have wronged you, and resist dwelling on the harm they caused. Instead, seek opportunities to bless them through your words and deeds.

Lastly, do not let your emotions dictate your response. Forgiveness is an act of the will, not merely a feeling. When your will aligns with God's, you open yourself up to abundant blessings from heaven. To illustrate the concept of forgiving in faith, I will share a personal example. I once had the privilege of working with a young lady who was experiencing severe migraines. As I interviewed her, she bravely shared a traumatic experience from her past – she had been abducted by an ex-boyfriend and subjected to sex trafficking. In the face of such a horrific ordeal, understandably, she was struggling with feelings of anger and resentment.

I felt conflicted about advising her on forgiveness, given the severity of her trauma. However, when I turned to prayer, seeking guidance from the Holy Spirit, I received a profound revelation. I realized that it wasn't about telling her to forgive in a way that negated the gravity of what had happened to her. Instead, the Holy Spirit led me to encourage her to forgive in faith.

As I explained to her, forgiving in faith does not diminish the reality of our pain; rather, it validates it. It acknowledges that yes, this hurt, and yes, this should never have happened. But forgiveness in faith is an act of submitting to the Word of God, an acknowledgment that while we might not fully understand the "why" we trust in the One who commands us to forgive.

I told her that forgiving in faith is a choice to release the right to hold on to our grievances, to lay down the heavy burden at the feet of the One who says, "Come to me, all who labor and are heavy laden, and I will give you rest" (Matthew 11:28).

It's an act of obedience that often runs counter to our human instincts for justice or retribution. It's a surrender, a choice to let God be the judge and to give ourselves the freedom to heal. Encouraging forgiveness in faith, especially in the face of such profound pain, allows individuals to find a path toward healing, restoration, and a renewed sense of purpose in their lives.

It's an acknowledgment of the power of faith and the transformative nature of forgiveness, even in the most challenging circumstances. To conclude the story, once she forgave the person, her migraine immediately ceased, and I have not received a report of her having another one, and this was over a decade ago.

Following the Great Forgiver

The journey of forgiveness is not one we embark on alone. We follow the footsteps of the Great Forgiver, Jesus Christ, who on the cross asked forgiveness for those who persecuted Him. In this ultimate act of mercy, we find our example and our strength.

Forgiving in faith is to live out the Gospel, to embody the grace we've been given, and to trust that in doing so, we open the door to a deeper healing—not just for ourselves but for the world around us.

We often rely heavily on logical and rational analysis, seeking explanations or justifications for every action or feeling to validate them. However, our human reasoning is prone to error, as it is limited by our earthly perspective. Moreover, our emotions can be influenced by our desire to maintain a certain self-image, whether it be high or low. To truly forgive, we must adopt God's perspective, as He is the ultimate Forgiver.

Jesus provided a parable to illustrate God's character and perspective on forgiveness. When Peter asked Jesus how many times he should forgive his brother, suggesting seven times, Jesus responded, "I tell you, not seven times, but seventy-seven times." He then shared the parable of a king settling accounts with his servants.

In the parable, a servant who owed the king an enormous sum, ten thousand talents, pleaded for patience and promised to repay everything. Despite the servant's inability to repay, the king had compassion and forgave the debt entirely. This story exemplifies God's boundless mercy and willingness to forgive, regardless of the magnitude of our debts.

By understanding and internalizing God's perspective on forgiveness, we can transcend our human limitations and extend forgiveness to others in the same manner as our Heavenly Father forgives us.

Following the master's act of compassion in forgiving his debt, thereby granting him freedom, the servant encountered another fellow servant who owed him a significantly smaller amount, a mere hundred denarii. In a sharp departure from the mercy he had just experienced, the forgiven servant aggressively grabbed his fellow servant and began to choke him, demanding immediate repayment.

Despite the debtor's pleas for leniency and assurance of repayment, the forgiven servant callously rejected his appeals. Instead, he callously had the debtor thrown into prison until the debt could be settled. This stark sequence of events vividly highlights the forgiven servant's hypocrisy and lack of compassion, as he failed to extend the same forgiveness to others that he had received himself.

Witnessing the unjust and merciless behavior of the forgiven servant towards his fellow servant deeply troubled the other servants, prompting them to report the incident to their master. Upon hearing the full account, the master summoned the forgiven servant and rebuked him harshly, condemning his wickedness and hypocrisy. The master reminded the servant of the immense debt that had been forgiven due to his pleading and questioned why he couldn't extend the same mercy to his fellow servant. In his anger, the master handed the forgiven servant over to the jailers to be tortured until he could repay his entire debt.

Through this parable, Jesus emphasizes the importance of forgiveness and warns of the consequences of failing to forgive others. He concludes by stating that this is how our heavenly Father will treat us unless we forgive others from our hearts. This serves as a powerful reminder of the significance of forgiveness in the eyes of God and underscores the necessity of extending mercy and compassion to others, just as we have received from Him.

The parable under discussion presents three crucial lessons. Firstly, it portrays God's capacity to absolve individuals of their debts, even when they may not merit such clemency. This profound forgiveness finds its ultimate manifestation in the sacrificial act on the cross, illustrating God's boundless grace.

Secondly, the parable underscores the significance of exercising our will to extend mercy to others. It emphasizes that forgiveness is not merely a passive response but a deliberate choice within our control. Lastly, the parable warns against harboring an unforgiving spirit, which incurs God's displeasure, especially among His children.

While there's a divergence of opinion, exemplified by Paula Sandford's assertion that forgiveness cannot be achieved solely through willpower, Scripture does not portray it as an insurmountable feat. Instead, it calls upon us to actively engage in the process of forgiveness rather than abdicating our responsibility to God.

The question is not whether we can forgive someone or not—we must forgive. But is it possible for us to forgive everything? Are we able to "forgive them for every wrong that they have ever done to us?" No, is the response. We can, however, extend forgiveness sparingly. God does not ask for more from us than we can provide.

He lets us start from where we are. For instance, from the time Linda was a child until he moved out of the house after graduation, Andrew had abused her. In general, Linda had often pardoned her brother for abusing her. But every time Linda spoke of Andrew, great anger would bubble up.

She never addressed him by his name. Forgiving her brother, Andrew, seemed an impossible task for Linda. However, after much contemplation, communication, and prayer, she found herself able to forgive him for the earliest remembered transgression. Initially, forgiveness was a daunting challenge.

Yet, as Linda gradually acknowledged Andrew's wrongdoings before God, forgiving him became easier with each passing incident. With time, Linda's anger dissipated as she forgave her brother for each offense over the years.

Eventually, her anger vanished entirely, and she began praying for Andrew's redemption. Upon her request, God, the heavenly Father, granted Linda, the victim of her brother's indiscretions, purification, leaving her feeling cleansed for the first time in her life. God desires us, His children, to reflect His character.

As Jesus emphasized, 'But I say to you who hear, love your enemies, do good to those who hate you, bless those who curse you, pray for those who mistreat you' (Luke 6:27-28). Achieving this requires extending forgiveness to our adversaries first."

In conclusion, forgiveness is a key that unlocks the chains of anger and hurt that binds our hearts. It's not always easy—indeed, it can be among the hardest things we ever do. But as we forgive in faith, obediently and trustingly, we align ourselves with the divine narrative that promises freedom and wholeness. We choose the path of healing, not just as a concept but as a lived reality, trusting in the Great Forgiver to transform our pain into a powerful testimony of His unending grace and love.

Other Spiritual Technologies for Healing

In addition to the powerful practice of forgiveness, the Bible offers a range of other spiritual techniques or technologies to address and resolve spiritual issues. These practices can lead to profound transformation and healing. Here are some key spiritual technologies mentioned in the Bible:

Prayer and Fasting

Jesus Himself emphasized the significance of prayer and fasting in addressing certain kinds of spiritual oppression. In Matthew 17:21, He mentions that certain spiritual challenges may only be overcome through prayer and fasting. This spiritual discipline involves seeking God through fervent prayer and abstaining from food or otherworldly distractions to draw closer to Him. It can lead to breakthroughs and a deeper connection with God.

Role of Prayer as Spiritual Discipline

Prayer is commonly understood as communication with God, often centered on our requests and needs. While this definition holds truth, there's a deeper dimension to prayer that's often overlooked.

In the book of Jeremiah, God extends an invitation to the Israelites: "Call to me and I will answer you and tell you great and unsearchable things you do not know" (Jeremiah 33:3). F. B. Huey Jr. highlights how this verse connects prayer with revelation, suggesting that divine insight becomes accessible when earnestly sought (referencing Matthew 7:7 and James 4:2–3).

Tim Keller expands on this idea, elucidating the profound link between prayer and God's revelation. He describes prayer as an ongoing dialogue initiated by God through His Word and grace, eventually culminating in a profound encounter with him. Keller emphasizes that the potency of our prayers lies not in our efforts or techniques but in our deepening understanding of God.

Donald Whitney echoes this sentiment, asserting that among all the Spiritual Disciplines, prayer ranks second only to the intake of God's Word in importance. This underscores the indispensable connection between prayer and Scripture. Without engaging with the Word of God, our prayers lack depth and resonance, akin to a one-sided phone conversation where we speak but cannot hear the other person.

In essence, prayer is more than mere supplication; it is a sacred dialogue with God, rooted in revelation through His Word, where our understanding of Him deepens and our communion with Him flourishes.

Engaging with Scripture and hearing from God has a transformative effect on us. However, a common question arises: does prayer have the power to change God? While the Bible doesn't explicitly state how our prayers influence God, it assures us that He hears us when we pray in accordance with His will (1 John 5:14). Considering this, our concerns about altering God's intentions through prayer diminish when we acknowledge that we wouldn't want Him to grant a request that isn't aligned with His perfect will.

With these considerations in mind, we can formulate a more comprehensive definition of prayer: Prayer is an intimate encounter with God, initiated by Him through His Word leading to profound changes within us. Through prayer, we humbly communicate with and worship the Lord, confessing our sins and shortcomings. We also petition Him to meet both our needs and the desires of our hearts. As we engage in this sacred dialogue, our hearts are transformed, and our relationship with God deepens.

The spiritual discipline of prayer holds significant importance, as highlighted by the Westminster Catechism's definition: "Prayer is an offering up of our desires unto God..." This concept finds biblical support in Jesus's words recorded in Matthew 7:7-8, where he assures us that if we ask, seek, and knock, God will respond generously. Indeed, God takes pleasure in answering the prayers of those who live uprightly (Proverbs 15:8).

However, there's a crucial caveat: Our desires must align with God's will. As the Westminster Catechism emphasizes, our requests should be "for things agreeable to his will." Thus, the essence of prayer lies in seeking alignment with God's purposes.

If the goal of spiritual disciplines is to mold us into godly individuals (as stated in 1 Timothy 4:7), then prayer serves as a crucial tool in achieving this transformation. Through prayer, we learn to surrender our will to God's, aligning our desires with His divine purposes. This discipline teaches us to echo the sentiment expressed by Jesus in Luke 22:42: "Not my will, but yours be done."

In essence, the primary purpose of prayer as a spiritual discipline is to guide us in conforming our hearts and minds to God's will, fostering a deeper intimacy with Him and allowing His purposes to shape our lives.

Here are Some Suggestions for Incorporating these Four Areas into your Prayers:

Adoration: Begin your prayer with adoration, expressing your love and reverence towards God. Focus on praising His attributes, His goodness, and His greatness. As R. C. Sproul suggests, let adoration be the starting point and increasing focus of your prayers.

Confession: After adoration, move into confession, acknowledging and admitting your sins before God. Be both general and specific, reflecting on your behavior over the past 24 hours and identifying particular instances of sin that need confession. Regularly ask the Holy Spirit to convict you of sin in your life.

Thanksgiving: Following confession, offer thanks to God for His blessings, especially those received daily. Choose at least three things to express gratitude for, such as eternal salvation, daily provision (e.g., food and clothing), and specific blessings experienced recently. Cultivate a heart of gratitude in your prayers.

Supplication and Intercession: Conclude your prayer with supplication and intercession. During supplication, bring your own needs and desires before God, asking Him for what you require. Simultaneously, engage in intercession, praying on behalf of others and their needs. Aim to include at least one request for yourself and one for someone else in every prayer.

By following this pattern, your prayers can encompass adoration, confession, thanksgiving, supplication, and intercession, fostering a deeper and more balanced relationship with God.

Why Should We Pray Every Day?

We Pray to Express the Depth of Our Daily Need for God: Prayer becomes a tangible expression of our profound dependency on God every day. As highlighted in John 15:5, Jesus emphasizes our interconnectedness with Him, likening Himself to a vine and us to branches. He underscores that apart from Him, we can accomplish nothing of eternal significance.

In essence, prayer serves as the intersection between our inherent inadequacy to navigate the Christian journey alone and God's boundless sufficiency to provide for our every need as His beloved children. It's a recognition that every facet of our existence hinges on God's grace, power, and provision.

Thus, the call to daily prayer extends beyond a mere routine; it's an invitation to cultivate a posture of continual, moment-by-moment reliance on God. In acknowledging our perpetual need for His intervention and guidance, we embrace the reality that even our ability to pray is a manifestation of His grace at work within us.

Daily prayer is not just a practice; it's a profound acknowledgment of our dependence on God's sustaining grace and a continual surrender to His sovereign will in every aspect of our lives.

We seek to delve into the depth of daily communion with God. Just before imparting what is commonly known as 'The Lord's Prayer' to his disciples, Jesus advised, 'And when you pray, do not babble on like pagans, for they think that by their many words they will be heard. Do not be like them, for your Father knows what you need before you ask Him' (Matthew 6:7).

God does not need reminders; He is already aware of our needs and takes pleasure in fulfilling them. The essence of prayer lies in the intimate connection established when one is alone with the Heavenly Father. Beyond mere desperation for things, there exists a profound yearning for a personal encounter.

In Exodus 33, we learn of Moses' encounters with God at the tent of meeting. Whenever Moses went out to commune with God, the people would rise and observe until he entered the tent. As the pillar of cloud descended, the people would worship, witnessing Moses' intimate communion with God 'face to face.' Even after Moses departed, his assistant Joshua remained at the tent (Exodus 33:7–11).

Picture the awe-inspiring scene: people standing in reverence as a man meets with God. Remarkably, we have the privilege of experiencing this communion moment by moment, day by day! By setting aside a regular time and place, we can partake in the blessings our Father has in store for us (Matthew 6:6)."

We pray to engage in the transformative power of serving God daily. Throughout the Bible, God extends promises to us through prayer, establishing it as a conduit through which we align ourselves with His divine purposes. As we engage in prayer, we witness His active involvement in our lives.

Our prayers do not seek to alter God's intentions or plans. It would be presumptuous for us, with our limited understanding, to attempt to impose our will upon the infinite wisdom of God. Instead, we place our trust in Him and express our deepest desires. The essence of prayer lies in seeking assistance from God while attributing all glory to Him (Psalm 50:15; John 14:13).

It is crucial to recognize that the effectiveness of prayer stems from God's power. Merely engaging in the act of prayer holds no inherent value. People from various religious backgrounds pray, but the significance lies in the recipient of our prayers. The power manifests when individuals connect with the Almighty God, transcending human limitations.

For those who belong to Christ, we are privileged to approach a Father who holds ultimate authority (Matthew 6:9), remains perpetually accessible (Psalm 27:8; 55:17), and continually operates within the world (John 5:17; Isaiah 40:28–31).

In a deeply spiritual and sincere connection with our Creator, God, we engage in a profound dialogue with him. Through prayer, we express our deepest emotions, share our joys and sorrows, and seek divine guidance. These moments of communion allow us to cultivate a close relationship with our Heavenly Father, finding comfort and strength amidst life's challenges.

Integrating Rest and Prayer

If mastering the spiritual practice of rest and prayer were effortless, I would have achieved it by now. However, like many aspects of life, it requires consistent prioritization and effort. While I don't claim to have all the answers, I can share some strategies that have proven effective in my journey of rest and prayer.

Commence with Surrender: True rest begins with surrender—a humble offering of our worries and cares to God through prayer. Although challenging, I recognize that God is capable of bearing the weight of the world. Prayer reminds me to intentionally set aside time each day to release my burdens, trusting in God's care.

Establish Sacred Spaces: Creating a designated space for communion with God is crucial. I've curated a peaceful environment in my home office with a comfortable chair, a small bookshelf, and soft lighting. This sacred space serves as a sanctuary for prayer and reflection, where I can find solace and engage in meaningful conversation with God.

Prayerful Rest: Recently, I experienced the tranquility of a cruise vacation, which provided ample opportunity for physical rest. Amidst the calm of the ocean, I found myself drawn to silent contemplation and prayer. Gazing at the vast expanse of water reminded me of God's boundless power and my need for His grace.

I encourage you to slow down and embrace the rest that comes from God's presence. By nurturing your soul and deepening your trust in our Heavenly Father, you'll discover a profound sense of peace and spiritual fulfillment.

Role of Fasting as Spiritual Discipline

In the intricate tapestry of our spiritual journey, fasting and prayer emerge as intertwined threads, creating a vibrant connection with God. This powerful combination transcends mere religious practice; it is a profound spiritual discipline deeply rooted in biblical teachings. As we explore of the transformative potential of fasting and prayer, it is essential to ground ourselves in the Word of God.

Throughout the Bible, we find numerous instances where fasting and prayer played pivotal roles in shaping the lives of individuals and communities. Jesus Himself set a profound example by undertaking a forty-day fast in the wilderness, highlighting the efficacy of fasting as a means of spiritual preparation and empowerment (Matthew 4:1-2). Similarly, the disciples engaged in fasting and prayer as they sought divine guidance for significant decisions (Acts 13:2-3).

Fasting is not about earning favor or manipulating God; rather, it represents a physical and spiritual posture of humility. As the psalmist David expressed during a time of repentance, "I humble myself with fasting" (Psalm 35:13b, NLT). Fasting prompts us to momentarily set aside our physical needs, acknowledging our reliance on God and surrendering our desires to His sovereign will.

Prayer serves as the heartbeat of our relationship with God. It is not merely a one-sided conversation but a dialogue through which we commune with our Creator. Jesus emphasized the potency of prayer in conjunction with fasting, declaring, "But this kind does not go out except by prayer and fasting" (Matthew 17:21, NKJV). Through prayer, we align our hearts with God's purposes and access His wisdom, strength, and grace.

Fasting is often likened to a spiritual cleanse, purifying our hearts and minds. Isaiah 58 vividly portrays the transformative effects of genuine fasting: breaking the chains of injustice, liberating the oppressed and extending aid to the needy. It transcends mere abstinence from food, urging active engagement in acts of compassion and justice.

James 4:8 urges believers to "Draw near to God, and he will draw near to you" (ESV). Fasting and prayer carve out a sacred space for us to approach God. By casting aside worldly distractions, we create room for a deeper, more intimate connection with God. In the stillness of fasting, we often discern the voice of God resonating within the depths of our souls.

Far from being outdated practices, fasting and prayer are timeless spiritual disciplines that propel us into God's presence. They serve as tools of transformation, guiding us toward spiritual growth and a deeper comprehension of God's intentions.

As we embark on this journey of fasting and prayer, let us heed Jesus' words in Matthew 6:18 (NLT), "Then no one will notice that you are fasting, except your Father, who knows what you do in private. And your Father, who sees everything, will reward you." May our fasting and prayers ascend as a pleasing offering, drawing us nearer to the heart of God.

Prayer and fasting are intricately linked, like two sides of the same coin, complementing each other perfectly. While prayer is the act of communicating with God, fasting involves purposefully refraining from food or other worldly pleasures for a set period to deepen and fortify the spiritual self.

By focusing on the needs of the spirit rather than the body, fasting aids in the growth and strengthening of faith. These practices can serve as powerful tools in addressing and overcoming our internal struggles.

Speaking God's Promises

Another powerful technique involves declaring and applying God's promises over one's life. This practice involves speaking biblical truths and affirming one's identity in Christ. Romans 8:1-2 assures believers that there is no condemnation for those in Christ who walk according to the Spirit rather than the flesh. By aligning one's thoughts and words with God's promises, individuals can break free from negative patterns and inherited issues.

Everybody has difficult days when they remove their rose-colored spectacles and see a half-empty glass in front of them. Let us say those days stretch into weeks, months, or years. Then what? It is difficult to break out from a negative cycle of thought.

Negative thought patterns have the power to go out of control and plunge us straight into the depths of despair. Feeling trapped and unable to look past what is directly in front of us is possible. But by bringing up the facts, we can get past poisonous thinking.

When we prioritize God's voice over negative thoughts, we sow seeds of goodness and vitality in the world. Aligning our mentality with God's word transforms positive thoughts into actions. Our daily choices form patterns that shape our realities.

By anchoring our beliefs in God's promises and affirmations, we empower ourselves to reshape our thinking. Through God's influence, our thoughts can be renewed, allowing us to speak truth into our circumstances.

An affirmation is a repeated remark or idea that one believes will bring about the desired outcome. It is not about realizing your destiny that these affirming messages and phrases are about. They do not focus on helping you attract your desires at the right time.

Do encouraging statements motivate people? Indeed. Do they motivate you? Naturally. Do they result in total fulfilment and change? My imagination is limited, and I have no idea what I do not know. It will not be to my ultimate benefit to try to attract the success that I have set for myself. It may give you a brief sense of satisfaction, but it is fleeting. The core is not addressed.

Sometimes the things we take for granted can have negative side effects and impede our ability to progress. Often, what we avoid might be the most beneficial and yield lasting contentment. Finding what we are all looking for will require much more than repeating phrases and thinking optimistically every day.

"Everything has its own beauty in the time appointed by Him. Yet, no one can grasp the full scope of God's work from beginning to end, despite His imprint of eternity on human hearts." - NIV Ecclesiastes 3:11

Each individual possesses a unique purpose and a path in life. We aren't meant to dictate our destinies alone. The Holy Spirit works tirelessly behind the scenes, guiding our lives with unparalleled potency. He comprehends the grand scheme and precisely understands His intentions for each of us.

These reassuring remarks and phrases serve as a reminder of biblical truths, which alter our perspective. They are about realizing that we require something much greater than ourselves. They have to do with learning to rely on the One who is able to supply our needs. They are about emptying oneself to make room for something greater, the Truth.

Our mental processes can be transformed by using biblical affirmations. God, not ourselves, should always be at the centre of our attention. Exodus 3:14 says, "He is I Am." He is everything and anyone we require. Only in I Am can we discover true satisfaction and prosperity in the long run.

"And people who recognise your name have faith in you." Psalm 9:10

When we need guidance, Jehovah Raah is our Shepherd. When we are in need, Jehovah Jireh is our Provider. In uncertain and uneasy times, he is Jehovah Shalom, the God of Peace. Jehovah Rapha is our Healer, the one we turn to when we need a solution to our broken circumstances or pain. When we need assistance navigating the challenges of life, Jehovah Nissi is our Banner.

Indeed, He is El Shaddai, the ultimate Source of blessings and the All-Sufficient One.

To affirm is to confidently declare the truth, and what better declarations to uphold than those affirming the presence of God in our lives! The word of God never returns empty (Isaiah 55:11); He watches over His word, ready to fulfill His promises (Jeremiah 1:12).

Regular meditation on scriptures is beneficial. As Joshua 1:8 instructs us, "Keep this Book of the Law always on your lips; meditate on it day and night, so that you may be careful to do everything written in it. Then you will be prosperous and successful."

True, enduring transformation results from matching scripture with our words, deeds, and attitudes according to Proverbs 18:21, a person's speech has the capacity to bring either life or death. We have the power to move mountains and comfort people with our words (Matthew 17:20; Proverbs 16:24). According to Romans 10:17, hearing the word transforms our entire worldview and fosters faith.

Paul, in Philippians 4:8, encourages us to focus on things that are noble and good, highlighting the importance of our thoughts and self-talk according to John 8:31–32, liberation from burdens, negative habits, doubt, and disappointment comes from embracing God's message.

Our thoughts and actions are interconnected, and our beliefs shape our thoughts. The key lies not in trusting ourselves above all else, but in placing our trust in God and embracing the transformation that occurs when we live in Him. Ultimately, it boils down to having faith that what He has spoken is true and will come to fruition.

Things that rely on God's promises will, and power must be affirmed. By reflecting on and uttering His message, we can see various facets of His nature that can support us throughout difficult times. Throughout every obstacle on our path, the Lord remains dependable and obedient. Speaking His word over our situation will allow Him to completely change us and make a way for us to follow.

Reversing Your Judgment

A unique spiritual technology introduced by Apostle Tony Kemp involves the concept of reversing your judgment. The Bible cautions against judgment, as in the passage "Judge not, lest you be judged" (Matthew 7:1). Apostle Kemp received the revelation that individuals can become spiritually bound or entangled with the same oppression, elements, or situations they judge.

When you start judging the person who is judging you, you are engaging in reverse judgment. Making such decisions might make one feel quite justified and even righteous—until they understand that they are both the same thing.

This is the reason Jesus states, "Judging those who judge you only makes room for the bitter root of judgment to be planted in your own heart." What then should a person do? Jesus encapsulates everything in two terms: Go from them.

Working with someone who knows everything is nearly impossible. What can be done when someone who is blind believes they can see clearly? Go from them. These individuals pose a threat. They are blind followers being led by blind leaders. That is the reason religious fundamentalism is so difficult to overcome. It is unaffected by outside interference. Go from them. It is time to let go of any lingering anger, give up the criticism that has caused you to become bitter, and finally wash your hands of them. Go from them.

Therefore, there is a need to reverse one's judgments through a process of repentance and forgiveness, breaking free from any negative spiritual attachments.

A remedy is sorely required in a world full of injustice, strife, misery, and bloodshed. Forgiveness is always available, yet it is so often disregarded or not even considered. Forgiveness seals what needs to be buried and removes what would otherwise fester, healing irreversible past wounds.

Despite what is commonly believed, forgiveness does not absolve someone of responsibility or allow wrongdoing to persist. Rather, it frees God's benefits from the shackles of pain and shame. We must forgive our sins of deceit and misdirection in order to remember that the best is yet to come. Forgiveness is the key to living a gracious life.

Reversing judgment is a profound spiritual concept that delves into the intricate dynamics of human interaction and the impact of our thoughts and actions on our spiritual well-being. Introduced by Apostle Tony Kemp, this concept carries significant weight, drawing from biblical teachings and offering a pathway to spiritual freedom and enlightenment.

At its core, reversing judgment entails a deliberate effort to break free from the negative spiritual repercussions that arise from passing judgment on others. This process involves several crucial steps designed to unravel the tangled web of judgment and pave the way for spiritual liberation.

The first step in reversing judgment is acknowledging one's own judgments. This requires introspection and self-awareness, as individuals must confront their biases, prejudices, and preconceived notions about others. Often, these judgments stem from deeply ingrained societal norms, personal experiences, or cultural influences. By acknowledging these judgments, individuals take the first step towards dismantling their hold over their spiritual consciousness.

The next step is releasing judgment. This involves letting go of the negative thoughts, attitudes, and emotions associated with one's judgments. It requires a conscious decision to relinquish the need to condemn or criticize others and cultivate compassion, empathy, and understanding instead. Releasing judgment is not easy, as it demands humility and a willingness to embrace vulnerability. However, it is a vital step towards spiritual growth and inner peace.

Seeking forgiveness and reconciliation is another crucial aspect of reversing judgment. When our judgments have harmed others, whether directly or indirectly, it is essential to take responsibility for our actions and seek reconciliation. This may involve apologizing to those we have judged, extending forgiveness to ourselves, and committing to fostering positive relationships based on mutual respect and acceptance. By seeking forgiveness and reconciliation, we not only mend broken relationships but also heal the wounds inflicted by judgment.

By undergoing this transformative process, individuals can strive for spiritual freedom and liberation. They break free from the chains of judgment that bind their souls, allowing them to experience a profound sense of inner peace and harmony. Moreover, reversing judgment enables individuals to cultivate a deeper connection with God and align themselves with the principles of love, compassion, and forgiveness espoused by spiritual teachings.

Crucially, reversing judgment also helps individuals avoid being ensnared by the same judgments they impose on others. By recognizing the interconnectedness of all beings and the biblical truth of reaping and sowing, individuals understand that the judgments they pass ultimately reflect back on themselves. As the adage goes, "What goes around comes around," and by releasing judgment, individuals break the cycle of negativity and sow good seeds.

In conclusion, reversing judgment is a transformative spiritual practice that empowers individuals to break free from the shackles of negativity and embrace a life of compassion, forgiveness, and love. It requires courage, humility, and introspection but offers the promise of spiritual liberation and enlightenment.

By acknowledging, releasing, and seeking forgiveness for their judgments, individuals can transcend their egoic tendencies and align themselves with the biblical principles of unity and interconnectedness. In doing so, they not only free themselves from the burden of judgment but also contribute to creating a more compassionate and harmonious world.

Inner Healing

While not explicitly mentioned in these terms, inner healing is a practice deeply rooted in biblical principles. It involves seeking healing and restoration for emotional and spiritual wounds. Inner healing often includes prayer, meditation on Scripture, and inviting the Holy Spirit to bring healing to past traumas, hurts, and negative emotions. It aligns with passages like Psalm 147:3, which speaks of God healing the brokenhearted and binding up their wounds.

Have you attempted many Christian forms of inner healing only to find that your spiritual problems or feelings remain the same? Why then does inner healing fail? What is the Bible's position on inner healing, then? Let us check it out!

The process involves confronting the immoral responses and false beliefs deeply rooted in our hearts due to life's traumatic experiences, often stemming from various sources but frequently intertwined with our parental relationships. Due to a lack of proper guidance in our formative years, we often react poorly, expressing thoughts or judgments that contradict our true values because we lack the tools to cope with adversity.

Given that everyone encounters pain in life, inner healing becomes a universal necessity. Failure to promptly and effectively address our emotional wounds results in prolonged suffering. Even when we attempt to suppress it, the pain lingers in our memories, affecting our earthly relationships and corroding our connection with God.

It impedes our capacity to love others and God as we should. Even if we grasp theological concepts and acknowledge God's love, hidden beliefs may linger within us, influencing our behavior contrary to our professed beliefs.

Even when told to the children, it is possible that they will not fully comprehend if the father of the family left to work since it was the only option to provide for the family. "Dad loves money more than me," they might be thinking.

Alternatively, people may swear within themselves, "I will never be poor." In twenty years, the usual outcome might be that one of the children is impoverished, driven to amass wealth, or has multiple divorces as a result. There are several ways something could go wrong. The adult children will probably find it difficult to put their trust in God to take care of their lives' in this regard.

When is inner healing necessary?

One of three things indicates that something in our hearts is not functioning:

- When we repeatedly run into the same bad circumstances or incidents in our lives.
- When we react strongly and excessively to something
- Every time we reflect on individuals or occasions that happened a long time ago, we experience new emotions.

I have put together a simple list of essential actions that are crucial for anyone receiving or facilitating inner healing. This is an essential component of the ministry of deliverance and is crucial in today's world of setting people free. God desires to take on your sadness, anguish, and wounds!

Before we start, I want you to know that God longs to remove our hurt and pain and mend our wounds. Do you know how it feels to love someone so deeply that you wish you could take away their sorrow or suffering? That is Jesus' opinion of each of us. He loved us so profoundly that He went to the cross to pay the price for our emotional recovery!

Isaiah 53:4 states, "Surely he hath borne our griefs, and carried our sorrows: yet we did esteem him stricken, smitten of God, and afflicted." This verse highlights that Jesus bore our sorrows on the cross. In the New Testament Greek, the word "sorrows" encompasses anguish, affliction, grief, pain, and sorrow. Jesus sacrificed Himself and shed His blood to pay the price for us.

The Bible reassures us of God's desire to heal our broken hearts and bind up our wounds, as stated in Psalms 147:3, "He healeth the broken in heart, and bindeth up their wounds." We are encouraged to cast all our cares upon the Lord because He cares for us (1 Peter 5:7). This includes releasing hurtful, painful, and fearful emotions into Jesus' hands.

Clutching onto fear, hurt, and pain can hinder the healing work of the Holy Spirit in our souls. Therefore, it's crucial to open up and allow the Lord to heal our wounds. Luke 4:18 emphasizes Jesus' mission to heal the brokenhearted, proclaim deliverance to captives, restore sight to the blind, and set free those who are bruised.

Jesus paid a significant price for the healing of our souls and to liberate us from bondage. It's essential to embrace this inner healing as it was obtained through His sacrificial offering.

Matthew 11:28–30 "All of you who toil and are burdened, come to me, and I will give you rest." 29 You will find rest for your spirits if you take up my yoke and learn about me. I am a humble and modest person. Because my burden is light and my yoke is easy. The verse above refers to a person's weight in their soul rather than a heavy physical load. The phrase "Ye shall find rest unto your souls" later in the passage makes this clear. Jesus is calling us to come to Him, to cast down our heavy loads, and to take up His light, manageable yoke.

As you entrust your painful emotions to the Lord, allow yourself to release them. It's okay to weep, cry, and pour out your wounded feelings into the hands of the Lord. Holding onto discomfort and hurt will only hinder your healing process.

James 5:16 advises, "Confess your faults to one another and pray for one another, that you may be healed." The earnest prayer of a righteous person has great effectiveness and benefit. Seeking support from a trusted confidant and receiving prayer for healing can be immensely helpful. Sharing your burdens with a fellow Christian brother or sister can facilitate healing.

Remember to acknowledge God's love for you, which will enable you to communicate with Him and experience inner healing. Understanding the real character of our heavenly Father will enable us to put our trust in Him and allow ourselves to be healed—a healing that can only be obtained via the power of the Holy Spirit.

Romans 8:32 states, "How shall he not freely give us all things with him who spared not even his own Son, but delivered him up for us all?" Why would Christ not heal our damaged spirits after He has suffered and died for us? Because of all He endured on the cross for us, we can safely open up to Him and know that He has our best interests at heart.

God loves you just for who you are, not for anything you have done. The Bible teaches that Christ died for us even though we were still sinners. Even before you were His child, He yearned for a relationship with you!

Romans 5:8 say, "But God commended his devotion toward us, in that Christ died for us while we were still sinners." According to Jesus, giving up one's life for friends is the greatest act of love a man can have for them. Jesus loved and cared for us so much that He gave His life for us!

"There is no greater love than this, that an individual lay down his life for his friends," says John 15:13.

Did you know that God's love for us is the same as His love for Jesus? Yes, this is true—believe it or not! Please find the following verse in the Bible: The world should know that you sent me and that you loved them just as much as you loved me, according to John 17:23, which states, "I in them, and thou one me, that they might be made perfect in one."

Understanding and experiencing the love of our heavenly Father is crucial for us to be filled with His fullness. Ephesians 3:17-19 emphasizes the importance of being rooted and grounded in love, comprehending the vastness of Christ's love, which surpasses human understanding, so that we may be filled with all the fullness of God.

Confronting the pain and emotional wounds within us with the healing love of Christ is essential. Recognizing that Jesus has already paid for our emotional wounds, hurts, pains, and sorrows, we can speak to these inner hurts, painful memories, and emotional afflictions, releasing them into Jesus' hands. We can pray for Jesus to remove these burdens from us and replace them with His peace.

The next step involves seeking deliverance from any spirits that may be influencing our minds or emotions. These spirits must be confronted and cast out in Jesus' name. This can be attempted as a self-deliverance or with the assistance of a qualified deliverance minister. If experiencing overwhelming or strong demonic reactions or if the spirits are not being expelled, seeking help from a qualified minister is recommended.

For those who are not yet believers in Christ, it is not advisable to confront evil spirits without first accepting Jesus as Lord and Savior. Without Christ, demons remain powerful spiritual beings, and confronting them can be dangerous. If you desire to accept Jesus as your Lord and Savior, you can pray a prayer of repentance and faith, inviting Him into your life to wash away your sins and transform you into a new person.

Worship and Praise

Engaging in worship and praise is another spiritual technology highlighted in the Bible. Worshiping God through music, songs, and expressions of gratitude can usher in the presence of God, bringing healing and deliverance. Psalm 22:3 states that God inhabits the praises of His people. Through worship, individuals can experience a shift in their spiritual atmosphere, leading to healing and breakthroughs.

Psalm 22:3 in the Bible states that He truly does dwell in our praises. This is the wonder and mystery of God's miraculous power and presence during worship! God's Word is confirmed to be true when we worship, and this affirmation is ingrained in our souls.

Engaging in worship holds an intrinsic power, offering us a profound connection to God's presence unlike any other. Advising individuals to merely cease worrying, displaying pride, indulging in self-absorption, succumbing to distraction, insecurity, bondage, or materialism proves ineffective.

Conversely, encouraging them to embark on a journey of worship proves transformative. Through worship, we gradually witness God's intervention, gradually loosening the grip of these inclinations as our focus shifts solely towards Jesus.

Worship is an expression of God's might and our frailty. In your next moment of need, I am challenging you to make the difficult decision to turn to worship and allow God to win the war on your behalf.

Worshipping involves the invisible God working powerfully and invisibly. We experience an incredible sense of calm and unspeakable joy as we are realigned, rejuvenated, and refueled. We learn about God's breakthrough strength, which gives us the ability to live in His presence, walk in the truth, and see Him win our fights.

Have you had this experience before? You seemed to be praying for someone to have a certain breakthrough, but nothing seemed to be occurring. When suddenly a "veteran of the faith" approached and started to pray, miracles happened. I prefer to refer to that individual as having spiritual authority. He is skilled in controlling evil spirits, entering the supernatural world, and staying in sync with the Holy Spirit (Galatians 5:25).

What distinguishes mature individuals from the inexperienced is their spiritual authority. Even if you currently perceive yourself as lacking influence in the supernatural realm, take the first step from where you stand. Embracing a steadfast commitment to follow Jesus forms the foundation and pinnacle of spiritual empowerment.

There are no shortcuts on this journey. Persist in being filled with the Spirit and confront challenges with unwavering trust in the potential for miracles. Let us refrain from timidly critiquing others and instead aspire, in the name of Jesus, to become towering figures of spiritual strength. Imagine the transformative impact of a worship team brimming with spiritual authority, fervently spreading the gospel message week after week!

Do not be a thermometer be a thermostat. It could be alluring to enter a space where indifference and discouragement are prevalent and then retreat out of fear. As worship leaders, we cannot afford only to reflect what we see in the space that we lead. If so, we cannot be the ones leading after all, can we?

Instead, let us step onto the platform with courage in our spirits, anticipation in our imaginations, and joy in our hearts as we partner with the Holy Spirit! The ability to elevate individuals to a new level of fervor is truly remarkable! Among all the points I've made thus far, this may be the most pertinent.

Happiness is truly contagious! Hope also spreads easily! If you are genuinely determined to lead with faith and excitement, people will gladly follow you! Yes, indeed! You will quickly be able to change the mood.

Confession and Repentance

Confession and repentance are essential spiritual practices in Christianity. As stated in 1 John 1:9, when we confess our sins, God's faithfulness and justice lead to forgiveness and cleansing from all unrighteousness. This foundational act of confessing and turning away from sin is instrumental in spiritual healing and restoration, allowing individuals to receive God's forgiveness and experience healing.

So turn from your sins and turn to God, repent, and the Lord will send you seasons of refreshing. – Acts 3:19

Do you want your sins to be washed and blotted away the way strong bleach and OxiClean can remove the dirtiest stains from your clothes? If so, turn to God and confess your sins. Nothing in this world, save trust in the purifying blood of Jesus alone, shed on the Cross, can cleanse you of the stains of your sin (1 John 1:7).

In Isaiah 43:25, God proclaims, 'I—yes, I alone—will erase your sins for my own sake and will never remember them again.' This divine act is fulfilled for all who repent and place their faith in His Son, who is the Lamb of God sacrificed for the sins of the world (John 1:29).

Are you feeling exhausted and burdened, longing for renewal? No amount of vacation time or sleep can compare to the rest and refreshment that Christ offers. Once more, repent and turn to God, for He is our Good Shepherd who sacrificed His life for His sheep; we lack nothing.

He guides us to lush pastures, leads us beside tranquil waters, and rejuvenates our spirits (Psalm 23). Is the Shepherd's voice drawing you near to Himself? Do not think twice about following Him. You may rely on Him, and He will provide you with sleep.

Accept His burden upon you and gain knowledge from Him; your spirit will find rest when you do. He is a kind and humble person. Because of this, His burden is light and His yoke is easy (Matthew 11:28-30).

Modify Your Opinion

The Greek word metanoia is where the word "repentance" comes from in the New Testament version of the Bible. This word denotes a shift in perspective and sentiment, moving away from sin and towards God along with His righteousness.

It includes a profound, sincere, and supernaturally enabled metamorphosis of one's beliefs, attitudes, speech, and actions. The key themes of the Apostles' preaching and teaching were conversion and trust in the Good News because they were also the central themes of Jesus' initial focus and declaration: "The time has come." "God's kingdom is almost here. Accept the gospel and turn from your sins! (Mark 1:15)

"In Luke 24:46-47, Jesus told his disciples, 'This is what is written: The Messiah will suffer and rise from the dead on the third day, and repentance for the forgiveness of sins will be preached in his name to all nations, beginning at Jerusalem.'

The Father, Son, and Holy Spirit delight in seeing people repent and receive forgiveness. It is through God's boundless love, grace, and mercy that we can repent and turn to Him for forgiveness. He is the one who bestows upon us repentance and eternal life, a gift that cannot be earned through our good deeds, as evidenced in the following scriptures:

'Opponents must be gently instructed, in the hope that God will grant them repentance leading them to knowledge of the truth.' (2 Timothy 2:25)"

"So then, to the Gentiles God provided repentance which leads to life," they praised God and said, having no more concerns after hearing this. Acts 11:18

"But even though we were dead in sins, God, who is rich in mercy, raised us alive with Christ because of his great love for us—you have been saved by grace." (Ephesians 2:1–4)

My immediate response to hearing the Good News was not one of faith and repentance. It took me nearly two years to come to terms with Jesus' identity and to change my opinion. And when I did, it was a real rebirth miracle. The Spirit of God, who is alive, became my source of power to live in accordance with His good, acceptable, and perfect will, replacing my heart of stone.

As I immersed myself in God's Word, my thinking underwent a transformation, aligning more closely with His teachings. The journey of progressive sanctification had commenced in my life. Uttering profanity no longer felt appropriate, and my previous sinful inclinations—idolatry, hatred, selfishness, and lust—became apparent as relics of my former sinful nature.

A profound sense of conviction regarding my sins emerged, accompanied by the empowerment to address them. The Holy Spirit began to illuminate the path of discipleship and ongoing repentance, reshaping my perspectives concerning God, humanity, myself, and the spiritual realm.

By God's grace, I was redeemed through the gift of repentance and faith, leading me to embrace the saving truth and enabling me to evade the snares of the Accuser (2 Timothy 2:24-26). The devil, also known as Satan—the 'accuser,' 'slanderer,' or 'adversary'—is the purveyor of falsehoods and the defeated ruler of darkness (Revelation 12:10; John 8:44; Colossians 2:15).

He is continuously enticing, blinding, and capturing people while being defeated, all the while holding them accountable to God for their disobedience and misdeeds. The devil also wants to prevent people from perceiving the gospel's light, which frees sinners from the dominion of darkness and their enslavement to sin and leads them to faith and conversion (2 Corinthians 4:4).

It is crucial to remember that you must persevere in walking in God's light and truth after having your eyes opened to the truth and light of the Gospel. The devil is a skilled trapper who will not give up on you easily. The devil will keep trying to ensnare you, but if you obey God and fight him, he will eventually go away from you (James 4:7).

Remember that "if we confess our sins, [God] is fair and just and will forgive us for our transgressions and purify us from all unrighteousness" (1 John 1:9) if you do fall into his trap and commit sin.

Hatred for Sin

Repentance embodies genuine remorse for our transgressions and a deliberate turning away from wrongdoing, coupled with a sincere commitment to abandoning our former sinful ways and embracing God by following Christ.

Faith in Christ isn't blind belief; it necessitates engaging our intellects with truth and historical evidence. Similarly, true repentance entails an intellectual acknowledgment that sin contradicts the teachings of the Holy Bible, God's Word. It entails a transformation of our understanding of good and evil, just and unjust, righteous and unrighteous, according to God's standards.

It involves cultivating a newfound aversion and grief for sin and lawlessness and making a personal choice to forsake it in favor of turning toward God. It entails relinquishing the gratification of our fleshly desires and instead embracing God's will, which brings Him pleasure. The Father God empowers and draws us to Jesus; it is His delight to summon sinners to repentance, an initiative He enables.

'No one can come to me unless the Father who sent me draws them, and I [Jesus] will raise them up at the last day.' (John 6:44). 'The Lord is not slow in keeping his promise, as some understand slowness. Instead, he is patient with you, not wanting anyone to perish, but everyone to come to repentance.' (2 Peter 3:9)

When we place our faith in Christ, we simultaneously turn away from the sin from which we ask Jesus to deliver us. Repentance and faith represent two distinct aspects of conversion, inseparable from each other. Saving faith cannot exist without repentance. Repentance is a beautiful, transformative, and life-saving process. It becomes a lifestyle for believers, signaling a new heart condition and disposition.

Christians do not repent once and then cease; an individual who repents and believes for the first time, experiencing profound forgiveness and salvation, will maintain that stance and attitude of repentance, faith, and reliance on God to overcome sin and the devil until the end. (Revelation 3:21)"

Worldly Sorrow and Godly Sorrow

Repentance transcends mere feelings of regret for mistakes and wrongdoing. Human sorrow, often triggered by being caught and facing consequences, typically revolves around self-interest and self-preservation. In contrast, genuine repentance, as articulated by Apostle Paul in 1 Corinthians 7:8-12, originates from godly sorrow.

This godly sorrow arises from recognizing our offenses against a supremely holy God and His image-bearers, leading to transformative repentance and purging our sins. The outcome of godly sorrow and repentance is a transformed life that brings glory to God and benefits ourselves.

In 1 Corinthians 7:10, Paul emphasizes that "godly sorrow brings repentance that leads to salvation and leaves no regret, but worldly sorrow brings death." This underscores the critical distinction between worldly and godly sorrow. While worldly sorrow may feign change and humility, only godly sorrow fosters genuine repentance and liberation from sin.

Paul further delineates the fruits of godly sorrow in verse 11: "See what this godly sorrow has produced in you: what earnestness, what eagerness to clear yourselves, what indignation, what alarm, what longing, what concern, what readiness to see justice done."

True repentance entails renouncing and forsaking all sins, pursuing justice fervently, and actively taking measures to avoid dishonoring God and repeating past transgressions. Conversely, worldly sorrow primarily manifests as self-pity stemming from exposure and the loss of approval or esteem in the eyes of others.

The Power of Repentance to Refresh

We are freed from the weight of our sin, shame, and guilt when we repent. We experience both God's peace and our own peace when we turn from our sins and accept the gospel of Jesus Christ. There is peace in our relationship with God. Our justification stems from our faith in the person, saving work, and resurrection of Jesus Christ.

This passage effectively interprets and contextualizes the biblical reference from Acts 3:19, providing insightful commentary on its meaning and significance within the broader biblical narrative. It highlights the connection between repentance, the outpouring of the Holy Spirit, and the ongoing work of refreshing and restoration initiated by God.

The explanation of the phrase "times of refreshing" and its potential fulfillment in the outpouring of the Holy Spirit adds depth and clarity to the interpretation of the verse.

Overall, this excerpt effectively combines biblical exposition with theological insight to convey a meaningful message about repentance and its spiritual implications.

The Greek word Anapsuxis is rendered as "refreshing" in English. This kind of regeneration cannot be found in a relaxing spa vacation or a cold glass of Coca-Cola on a hot day. It is not simply any ordinary refreshment.

Acts 3:19's Greek word Anapsuxis can be explained as follows: Psuxis, which means "breath," "soul," or "life" in Greek and denotes our deepest being—the source of our thoughts, volition, and emotions—and ana, which normally means "again" or "re" in Greek, frequently signifying repetition. When used together, anapsuxis means "recovery of breath" and "refreshment" or "revival of the soul."

The Lord bestows spiritual renewal or revival upon those who turn away from their sinful ways and accept Jesus Christ, the Messiah, for salvation. Through His Spirit (referred to as "pneuma," which also signifies wind or breath in Greek), God breathes new life into the human soul, providing a revitalizing surge of vitality.

Thus, according to biblical teachings, genuine repentance and faith in God lead to purification from sin and a supernatural revitalization of the inner being, influencing thoughts, speech, actions, and ultimately shaping the eternal course of our lives. Truly, all glory and praise belong to the triune Godhead, who graciously grants repentance, purification, and His rejuvenating presence to undeserving sinners.

In the pursuit of emotional and spiritual healing, it's important to recognize that these practices can complement other spiritual technologies. They work in tandem with forgiveness, prayer, fasting, and the application of biblical truths. By integrating these practices into our spiritual lives, we open ourselves to transformation, breakthroughs, and a deeper connection with God.

Moreover, as we navigate the complexities of emotional and spiritual healing, we must understand that some knots in our lives can be addressed through confession and repentance.

When we have harmed others or violated our own values, acknowledging our wrongs, seeking forgiveness, and making amends can be integral to the healing process. Confession and repentance, in conjunction with other spiritual practices, can untangle even the most deeply ingrained knots, paving the way for spiritual wholeness and growth.

Confession and repentance are foundational aspects of the healing journey, primarily directed towards God as we seek His forgiveness and restoration. However, it's essential to recognize that we are also instructed to take direct steps in resolving harm or offenses with the individuals involved. Failing to do so can sometimes strengthen and tighten the knots that bind us.

Consider the example of a young man I once counseled who was grappling with a knot of anxiety and fear. Anxiety can be paralyzing, making it challenging to seek immediate counsel or assistance. During such times, it becomes crucial to pray for patience and guidance, both for ourselves and those we aim to help.

In this specific case, I encouraged the young man to reach out to individuals who could provide a safe space for him to share his experiences. It's important to remember that when someone approaches you for help, they may repeatedly express their concerns, almost like a broken record. This repetition can be a vital part of the process of untangling the knots within them, even if they aren't fully aware of it.

In the example I mentioned, the individual eventually revealed that they had been unfaithful to their partner, and the guilt was consuming them. I advised them that they had identified the source of their knot and the choice to address it with the person they had harmed was ultimately theirs to make. It's worth noting that some well-meaning individuals might suggest not confessing, citing God's forgiveness.

Admittance is undoubtedly essential for the initiation and progression of recovery. To confess is to consent to reality. We acknowledge our imperfections. We acknowledge that we have an issue. We acknowledge that we are weak and unable to overcome our mistakes and shortcomings on our own. Every time we acknowledge that our beliefs or behaviors do not align with what God has declared to be good or just, we are agreeing with the truth.

Confession serves as an authentic acknowledgment and articulation of truth. However, confession by itself does not bring about behavioral change. While confession opens the door for God's forgiveness and purification into our shattered lives, repentance truly alters the trajectory of our recovery in the long term.

Repentance is the act of turning away from anything that is contrary to the truth. Confession is balanced with repentance. We repent—that is, we turn away from the oppositional idea, belief, or behavior that led to the confession—after confessing our agreement with the truth. We teach our hearts and minds to focus on truth—the path that leads to freedom and life—through repentance.

Furthermore, as we keep moving in the direction of truth, we see God's might unleashed against the deceptive ideas, attitudes, and deeds that aim to drag us back into the depths of shame, darkness, and hopelessness.

Pride poses one of the most significant obstacles to repentance. It deceives us into believing that we know what's best for our lives, even when it may lead to our downfall. Instead of humbling ourselves and surrendering to the truth of God's Word and His ways through repentance, we often try to rationalize our way out of the sinful traps we find ourselves in, particularly those fueled by lust.

Though a hideous force, pride often goes unnoticed as we wriggle and squirm away from the loving invitation of repentance and a new way of life. However, to truly transform into a new individual, a liberated and pure child of God, we must relinquish our pride and willingly embrace the path of repentance.

A detrimental foe of repentance is the reduction of our sin. We trick ourselves into thinking that we can effectively handle our sexuality on our own and that our difficulties are not as serious as they actually are. We claim we are not harming anyone or that we just have a "small" problem with porn. The more time we spend fanning the flames of arrogance and minimization, the more we will stray from confession and pay the price.

Confession holds significant importance in the recovery process. However, without repentance, confession merely serves to repeatedly acknowledge the same wrongdoing without actively seeking to address it.

Repentance complements confession by directing us towards the right mindset and perspective after experiencing the revitalizing cleansing brought about by sincere confession. Therefore, it's essential to let your moments of confession prompt you to take the additional step towards long-term freedom by embracing repentance. This journey is the pathway to genuine and lasting freedom.

However, it's essential to remember that the act of confession and reconciliation can bring about healing not just for the person offering it but also for the wounded relationship and the person who was wronged. Through these steps, we begin to untangle the knots that hinder our spiritual and emotional growth.

A Lifelong Journey of Untangling Knots

Furthermore, our personal journeys in faith often intersect with these complex knots. Allow me to share a personal example from my own life when I was younger. I struggled with an incessant itch on my legs that seemed to intensify after getting wet. It was a perplexing and uncomfortable issue that had no apparent physical cause. However, through prayer and seeking spiritual insight, I came to a startling revelation: this uncontrolled itch might be a manifestation of a generational curse that had been passed down through my family.

This realization struck a chord with me, especially when my older brother shared that he was dealing with the same inexplicable itch. It was a powerful reminder of the interconnectedness of our lives and experiences within our familial context. But it was also a moment of hope and revelation. I fervently prayed and sought deliverance, and through God's grace, the itching ceased. It was a tangible example of how addressing the spiritual knots in our lives, even those with deep generational roots, can lead to healing and freedom.

Indeed, untangling these knots is a lifelong journey. It necessitates unwavering dedication to spiritual disciplines, a willingness to seek guidance from the Holy Spirit, and the application of the powerful tools that God's Word provides.

As 2 Corinthians 10:4 reminds us, 'For the weapons of our warfare are not carnal but mighty in God for pulling down strongholds.' Additionally, my experience with the itch draws parallels with Deuteronomy 28:35, which speaks of discomforts that may be linked to generational issues, emphasizing the importance of seeking spiritual resolution.

In summary, the origins of our inner knots may be as ancient as our family lineages, but the solutions are timeless, rooted in the transformative power of forgiveness and the liberating truths found in the Word of God. Through these spiritual practices, there is hope and potential for freedom, not just for the individual but for generations to follow."

Chapter 2:   **The Nature of Memories**

In this chapter, let's dive into the world of memories, shall we? It's a bit like pondering the mysteries of the universe. How long does a memory stick around? Does it have a clear beginning and end?

And what's the deal with memories flashing before people's eyes on the brink of death? Is it our body's way of making sense of it all? You see, memories are like the mile markers of our daily lives. They silently influence our routines, decisions, and emotions. But it can be pretty disorientating when they start slipping away, like forgetting important dates or events.

Here's a fascinating twist – the memory journey begins even before we're born! Research indeed supports the notion that babies begin forming memories even before birth. While the exact mechanisms and intricacies are still being studied, there is evidence to suggest that prenatal memory development is a real phenomenon.

One study published in the Proceedings of the National Academy of Sciences in 2010 found that unborn babies, as early as 30 weeks gestation, were capable of forming memories of sounds they had been exposed to repeatedly while in the womb. This indicates that babies can start recognizing and remembering certain auditory patterns before they are born.

Another study, published in the journal Infant Behavior and Development in 2019 showed that unborn babies can remember and react to maternal speech sounds. The researchers found that fetuses responded differently to familiar and unfamiliar speech sounds, suggesting that they were capable of distinguishing between them.

These studies, among others, shed light on the remarkable capacity of unborn babies to begin processing and retaining information even before they enter the world. The implications of these findings underscore the importance of maintaining a positive and stress-free environment during pregnancy, as it can contribute to the healthy development of a child's early memories and emotional well-being.

As we start building memories before we enter the world, it is worth pondering the relevance of how they govern our lives. Let's untangle the threads of memory together, exploring how they shape our lives, from the faintest recollections to the most vivid moments.

For instance, I can't readily remember what I had for breakfast just two days ago. Why? It's not because breakfast is an insignificant part of my day; it's because most breakfasts I've had over the past four decades have been uneventful.

But there are those breakfasts that stand out, like the one when my father picked up my siblings and me and took us to have breakfast before a visit to the zoo. This memory is etched into my mind because it was a rare and positive experience with my father, someone I was not raised with. It's one of the few life-altering moments I shared with him while I can recall a few other impactful breakfasts, most simply concluded as neutral memories.

Through this chapter, my hope is to guide you on a journey toward healing from the traumas of your past by exploring possible unresolved memories that might hinder your ability to be fully present. It's essential to note that I am not a psychologist, and I won't be providing medical advice.

I am a novice researcher with a strong biblical foundation, and I believe that this foundation is key to discovering the answers we often seek. I do advise that you engage with this book while keeping in mind the importance of seeking professional counselors when necessary. As the Bible wisely states, "Where there is no counsel, the people fall, but in the multitude of counselors, there is safety."

The brain tends to retain highly emotional memories longer compared to neutral memories. Negative memories, in particular, tend to linger because they are associated with high-stress situations. This retention of negative memories serves an evolutionary purpose, as it helps individuals recognize and avoid similar stressful situations in the future.

Have you ever pondered over how past memories, especially the negative ones, influence your present state? Picture yourself in a peaceful moment when the memory of a past failure, such as a botched presentation, suddenly intrudes, disrupting your tranquility.

You might notice physical reactions like sweaty palms, an increased heart rate, and a churning stomach, followed by a familiar sense of dread. Interestingly, this experience is not unique to you; everyone sometimes grapples with revisiting old negative thoughts.

Scientific inquiry into the nature of negative thoughts has been ongoing for years. In 2006, researchers Elizabeth Kensinger from Boston University and Daniel Schacter from Harvard University conducted a notable study on emotional memory recollection. Their research centered on the 2004 American League Championship series between the Boston Red Sox and the New York Yankees, chosen for its high emotional intensity.

The study grouped participants into three categories: highly positive (Red Sox fans), highly negative (Yankees fans), and neutral (those not fans of either team). The findings revealed that individuals emotionally invested in the outcome of the event—either due to their team winning or losing—recalled the details more vividly than neutral observers.

Interestingly, the negative group (Yankees fans) displayed even sharper recall than the positive group (Red Sox fans), indicating that negative memories are not only more vivid but also less susceptible to distortion compared to positive memories.

Another study in 2007 examined the emotional impact of the fall of the Berlin Wall. Participants were divided into groups based on their emotional response to the event—positive or negative. Results showed that those with a negative perception of the event exhibited more accurate recollections than those with a positive outlook.

Subsequent research corroborated these findings, demonstrating that emotional memories are retained with greater precision than non-emotional ones. This underscores the significance of remembering emotional experiences, as they contribute to our understanding and adaptation to the world.

To comprehend why the brain tends to retain emotional experiences better, it's essential to delve into the mechanisms of memory storage in the brain.

At the core of memory processing lies the hippocampus, a small structure nestled within the temporal lobe. This region plays a pivotal role in consolidating our long-term memories, among its various functions. However, the formation and recall of emotional memories engage the hippocampus, the amygdala and certain areas of the prefrontal cortex.

The amygdala, resembling a small almond, holds sway over our emotional responses, particularly those linked to fear and aggression. During the recollection of an emotional event, the amygdala contributes the emotional nuances, with greater intensity corresponding to the strength of the emotion felt.

Additionally, various segments of the prefrontal cortex, associated with emotional regulation and social conduct, contribute to shaping our emotional memories. These structures, often interconnected with the limbic system, the brain's seat of emotions, play a significant role in processing emotional experiences.

Researchers speculate that the joint involvement of the amygdala and the prefrontal cortex in emotional memory retrieval facilitates the recall process. The activation of neurons in these regions by emotional stimuli prompts them to transmit signals to the hippocampus. This influx of signals to the hippocampus is believed to reinforce the encoding and retention of the memory. However, the precise neural pathways underlying emotional memory retrieval remain a subject of ongoing investigation.

While emotional memories hold considerable sway over our recollection, negative memories, in particular, wield a profound impact. The dominance of negative memories might seem perplexing, but the explanation lies in their potent emotional charge and the evolutionary imperative to prioritize threat avoidance.

Research findings illustrate that rats have the ability to recall specific locations in experimental settings where they experienced a shock. Functional magnetic resonance imaging (fMRI) scans conducted on participants prompted to recollect emotional experiences revealed heightened activity in regions of the brain, including the hippocampus, amygdala, and various parts of the prefrontal cortex, particularly when recalling negative events.

Negative events typically induce stress responses in the body, releasing stress hormones such as epinephrine and cortisol. Studies utilizing positron emission tomography (PET) and fMRI have demonstrated the pivotal role of stress hormones in modulating and reinforcing memory through their action on the amygdala.

Epinephrine and cortisol are believed to exert their effects primarily on the basolateral amygdala (BLA), which plays a critical role in storing fear-conditioned responses. Consequently, the heightened release of these hormones during negative experiences contributes to the enhanced encoding and retrieval of negative memories. The amygdala becomes notably activated, sending potent emotion-laden signals to the hippocampus, resulting in the vivid recollection of negative incidents both in terms of memory and emotion.

The question arises as to why our physiology prioritizes the consolidation of negative memories despite their distressing nature. Scientists propose that this phenomenon carries evolutionary significance, as the ability to recall negative events serves as a survival mechanism. In ancestral environments, where threats to life were prevalent, the capacity to remember and avoid potential dangers conferred a distinct survival advantage.

However, in contemporary society, the nature of negative events has evolved to encompass various stressors, such as academic setbacks or traumatic experiences unrelated to physical peril. Despite this shift, the underlying mechanism of memory consolidation remains geared toward enhancing survival prospects by learning from past adversities.

Individual differences in the degree of recollection of negative events can be attributed to variations in the release of stress hormones and the unique patterns of mnemonic encoding in each person. Nonetheless, it's important to note that humans are not solely inclined to recall negative experiences; moments of joy and cherished memories are also stored in the hippocampus, often resistant to memory distortion.

The enduring impact of negative memories, though perceived as burdensome, can be reframed as an adaptive response shaped by evolution. Rather than being a source of perpetual distress, these memories serve as valuable lessons, equipping us to navigate future challenges with greater resilience and foresight.

As we delve into the realm of memories, I challenge you to process these thoughts with me. I believe that through open and critical exploration, you may glean insights from my personal experiences, which I share with the intention of assisting you.

While our individual situations may not be identical, I am confident there will be enough similarities for you to allow the Holy Spirit to guide your journey. I encourage you to pray for specific insight regarding your next steps, as they may or may not align with the ones, I personally took to resolve my memories.

Neutral Memories and Their Impact

Life is a complex quilt composed of memorable moments and experiences, yet there exist vast stretches of time, neutral memories, that go unnoticed and uncelebrated. These hours of our lives are often overshadowed by the grand events, but they also have their own significance.

Neutral memories are many hours of your life that are often inaccessible due to their level of repetition or their being uneventful, which is not to be confused with suppressed memories. In this exploration, we will delve into the world of neutral memories, understanding their importance, their impact on our lives, and how they are intertwined with biblical references.

As previously written, neutral memories encompass the ordinary and unremarkable aspects of our daily lives. They are the routines, the mundane, and the seemingly insignificant moments that we tend to overlook. These memories often fall into the background as our minds prioritize the more exciting or emotionally charged events.

"Life is made up of an infinite number of moments, good and bad. Those neutral moments are the glue that holds it all together." - Unknown

One of the defining characteristics of neutral memories is repetition. Repetition can lead to a sense of monotony, making it easy to dismiss these moments. However, it is important to recognize that it is within these repetitive experiences that we find consistency and stability in our lives. Repetition provides structure, and structure can offer a sense of security and comfort. Another aspect of neutral memories is their perceived lack of excitement.

These moments may seem uneventful, but they form the backdrop against which the more dramatic events of our lives play out. They offer respite and balance, allowing us to appreciate the extraordinary when it does occur. From a psychological standpoint, neutral memories are essential for our mental well-being. They provide a sense of continuity and stability in our lives. Psychologists have long recognized the value of routine and predictability in reducing stress and anxiety.

The Significance of Positive Memories

Positive memories are the treasures of our past, the emotional snapshots that bring us joy, peace, and a deep sense of contentment when we revisit them. These memories hold within them the power to shape our perspectives and influence our future endeavors. In this exploration, we will delve into the significance of positive memories, backed by research, quotes, and biblical references, to illuminate their role in fostering a positive outlook on life, even in the face of future challenges.

Positive memories, often intertwined with moments of happiness, achievement, and love, serve as emotional anchors in our lives. They remind us of our capacity for joy and resilience, helping us navigates the complexities of life with optimism.

Reflecting on positive memories and revisiting them can profoundly impact our emotional well-being, offering a glimpse into the good times we've experienced and the potential for future happiness through our efforts.

What is it about revisiting a happy memory that brings a smile to our faces? Perhaps it's the people we shared that moment with, the joyous occasion itself, or the sheer perfection of the moment - the right place, time, and company.

The poet John Keats eloquently described such moments as "Moments big as years," emphasizing their lasting impact on our lives. These moments, rich with emotional significance, imbue our lives with purpose and joy, continuing to uplift us long after they've passed. They are a source of enduring happiness, a precious gift that keeps on giving. Actively recalling positive memories contributes to greater life satisfaction and enjoyment.

Studies have shown that intentionally reflecting on and reliving happy memories leads to higher levels of contentment and satisfaction compared to those who do not engage in such practices. Nostalgia, characterized by sentimental fondness for the past, has been identified as a potent enhancer of happiness. It has the remarkable ability to bolster one's sense of self, amplify positive emotions, and serve as a shield against negative thoughts.

Indeed, the ability to fondly reminisce about past experiences, relationships, and moments of joy can significantly enhance overall well-being. Happy memories have the power to bring warmth and comfort when we need it most, reminding us of the beauty and positivity that life has to offer.

Positive emotions: Photographs serve as precious treasures, instantly transporting us back to joyful moments from our past. These images, whether of our families, we, or others, can evoke memories more swiftly than magic. They not only preserve moments from our past but also offer countless happy recollections each time we revisit them. Whether they elicit laughter, tears, or a desire to share, photographs almost always evoke a positive response.

Stress Reduction: Happy memories serve as a lifeline during stressful periods in our lives. Reflecting on past successes, family vacations, or moments of laughter can energize us and propel us forward in a positive direction. This reflection triggers a relaxation response, lifts our spirits, and diminishes worry.

Increases sense of gratitude: Recalling happy memories often evokes feelings of gratitude. These positive mood shifts can linger throughout the day, fostering a deep sense of appreciation for life and our surroundings.

Increases self-esteem: Remembering moments of great happiness and accomplishment is often linked to periods of success. Whether it's being recognized as the top student or receiving praise for a job well done, such joyful recollections inspire us to strive for excellence and bolster our self-esteem.

Relationship satisfaction: Happy memories shared with loved ones strengthen emotional and social bonds, fostering a greater sense of community and connection.

Health Benefits of Recalling Good Memories: Revisiting happy memories offers numerous health benefits beyond momentary joy. Studies indicate that purposefully recalling joyful memories can help break negative thought patterns, reduce anxiety, and lower cortisol levels. This practice has proven particularly effective in improving the mental well-being of individuals at risk for depression due to stress.

Improved sleep: Focusing on happy memories before bedtime can redirect our thoughts from negative to positive, improving both the quantity and quality of sleep.

Immune system functioning: Positive memories have been shown to enhance immune system function, increasing antibody production and reducing inflammation, thereby promoting overall health.

Cardiovascular functioning: Recalling happy memories regulates blood flow and improves heart health, mitigating the negative impact of stress on the cardiovascular system.

In conclusion, harness the power of your memories! Cherish those "moments big as years," keeping them close to your mind and heart to infuse your life with greater joy whenever needed.

"Positive thinking will let you do everything better than negative thinking will." – Zig Ziglar

Positive memories have been the subject of extensive research in psychology. Studies show that recalling positive memories can have profound effects on our mental well-being. Revisiting these memories can lead to increased feelings of happiness and reduced stress levels. They serve as a reservoir of emotional strength, helping us face the future with a brighter perspective.

Biblical References: "Finally, brothers and sisters, whatever is true, whatever is noble, whatever is right, whatever is pure, whatever is lovely, whatever is admirable—if anything is excellent or praiseworthy—think about such things." – Philippians 4:8.

Nurturing Positivity through Positive Memories

Our collection of positive memories is like a garden; it requires cultivation. Regularly revisiting these memories can be a deliberate act of self-care. It reminds us of the beauty in our lives and reinforces our ability to overcome challenges.

"A good memory is one that can remember the day's blessings and forget the day's troubles." – Unknown

Creating and cherishing new positive memories is equally important. Engaging in activities that bring us joy, spending time with loved ones, or pursuing our passions can contribute to building a repository of positive experiences that will serve as valuable resources in the future.

Research on Positive Memory Enhancement: Studies suggest that practicing gratitude, mindfulness, and keeping a journal of positive experiences can enhance our ability to recall and benefit from positive memories.

Biblical References: "Give thanks in all circumstances; for this is the will of God in Christ Jesus for you." – 1 Thessalonians 5:18

The Bible is a source of wisdom, comfort, and courage for many individuals, offering verses that bring serenity and guidance during difficult times. Some of these verses specifically address happiness, providing insight and encouragement for maintaining a positive outlook.

The Bible also underscores the importance of righteousness and joyful living. In John 10:10, Jesus speaks of abundant life, highlighting the potential for joy and fulfillment in living to the fullest extent. This verse suggests that life encompasses more than mere existence—it involves pursuing happiness while upholding moral values.

While the terms "joy" and "happiness" are often used interchangeably, they can carry distinct meanings culturally. Happiness may be perceived as either a fleeting emotion of joy or a long-term state of contentment, well-being, and satisfaction.

Joy typically refers to an emotional state, while happiness can denote a sense of overall satisfaction. Happiness is often linked to external factors that bring pleasure, whereas joy can arise internally, prompted by both external and internal events.

In Christianity, the Bible emphasizes joy rather than happiness. Although the term "happiness" is seldom found in the Bible, joy is a prevalent theme. Jesus Christ advocated for inner peace and joy, discussing salvation and redemption through joy and peace even amidst adversity. By focusing on God and eternity, Christians are encouraged to find happiness in challenging circumstances.

While life presents its share of challenges, these obstacles need not preclude lasting happiness. Many find solace and joy through practices like self-care, self-forgiveness, and immersion in scripture. By seeking guidance from the Bible and nurturing a relationship with God, individuals can cultivate a deeper sense of joy and fulfillment, even in the face of adversity.

The Healing Power of Positive Memories

The Healing Power of Positive Memories is a concept that highlights the transformative potential of focusing on and embracing the positive aspects of our past experiences. In the fabric of our memories, negative events often loom larger than positive ones, casting a shadow over our perception of life's journey.

This imbalance can perpetuate a cycle of suffering as the negative memories dominate our thoughts, emotions, and actions, distorting our self-image and influencing how we navigate new challenges.

However, by consciously acknowledging and resurrecting positive memories, we can begin to shift this paradigm. Positive memories serve as reservoirs of resilience, offering solace and strength during difficult times.

They remind us of moments of joy, love, and accomplishment, illuminating the darker recesses of our minds with their radiant light. When we intentionally recall these uplifting experiences, we loosen the grip that negative memories have on our psyche, allowing us to cultivate a more balanced and healing perspective.

By tapping into the power of positive memories, we reclaim agency over our narrative, rewriting the script of our lives with a focus on resilience, gratitude, and hope. These memories become anchors that ground us amidst life's storms, providing stability and reassurance as we navigate the unpredictable waters of existence.

Moreover, they serve as catalysts for growth and transformation, inspiring us to persevere in the face of adversity and to embrace the full spectrum of human experience.

In essence, the healing power of positive memories lies in their ability to transcend the limitations of our past traumas and to illuminate the path towards healing and wholeness. By embracing and cherishing these moments of brightness amidst life's challenges, we empower ourselves to create a future filled with possibility, resilience, and joy.

The Full Picture of Our Life Situations

Negative memories often act as blinders, leading us to fixate on what has gone wrong, and in doing so, we neglect the full scope of our experiences. By allowing positive memories to surface, we allow ourselves the opportunity to have a more complete and nuanced understanding of our life situations. This broader perspective can alleviate the impact of traumatic memories and assist in constructing a narrative that includes resilience, growth, and the capacity for happiness.

The Role of Positive Memories in Scripture

The Bible often points to remembrance as a source of encouragement. In Psalm 147:3, the psalmist speaks of God as one who "heals the brokenhearted and binds up their wounds." This healing is not just a spiritual or physical act but also an emotional one where the recollection of God's past faithfulness can be a salve for present hurts.

Similarly, Lamentations 3:21-23 encourages us to call to mind the Lord's mercies, which are new every morning, as a reason for hope. These scriptures advocate for a trust in God's ongoing provision and imply a reflection on the good that has been and can be experienced.

The quote from Nelson Mandela, "The greatest glory in living lies in never falling, but in rising every time we fall," encapsulates the power of positive remembrance. It's not about the absence of failure or pain but about the ability to overcome and rise again. Mandela's life itself is a testament to the power of a positive outlook, as his resilience and forgiveness in the face of tremendous adversity have inspired millions.

In conclusion, embracing the full breadth of our memories, both positive and negative, leads to a more holistic self-awareness and emotional health. The practice of recalling positive memories is not about denial of the negative but about affirming the good that has been part of our journey. This practice can lead to a more balanced narrative of our lives, wherein each memory, positive or negative, is given its due place and influence, allowing us to move forward with a sense of wholeness and hope.

Positive memories are not just fleeting moments of joy but the building blocks of a positive and resilient mindset. Backed by research, reinforced by wise quotes, and grounded in biblical wisdom, these memories have the power to sustain us through life's challenges.

 As we continue to cultivate and nurture our positive memories, we are better equipped to face the future with hope, knowing that our past is filled with moments of joy, love, and triumph. In embracing the power of positive memories, we find the strength to navigate life's uncertainties with optimism and resilience. We cultivate a brighter and more hopeful future by tending to our emotional garden.

"Remember the past with gratitude. Live the present with enthusiasm. Look forward to the future with confidence." – Saint John Paul II

Understanding and Addressing Suppressed Memories

Memories are like pieces of a puzzle that make up the story of our lives. But what happens when some of these puzzle pieces is missing or hidden away? Suppressed memories, a fascinating and somewhat mysterious aspect of our inner world, have intrigued psychologists and everyday people for years.

What Are Suppressed Memories?

When discussing repressed memories, we are referring to a defense mechanism employed by the mind to suppress unwanted memories. As conceptualized by Sigmund Freud in his psychoanalytic theory, repression is a mechanism by which certain memories or experiences are pushed into the unconscious mind. This theory falls within the realm of talk therapy modalities.

To comprehend repression, it's essential to understand the conscious, preconscious, and unconscious mind. The conscious mind holds information and ideas that we are currently aware of. The preconscious mind stores information and memories that we are not actively using but can recall when needed.

The unconscious mind contains information that we cannot access and that we are not consciously aware of. With repression, memories that are perceived as frightening, painful, humiliating, or unacceptable are pushed from the conscious or preconscious mind into the unconscious mind. This process results in individuals being unable to recall specific memories because they have been securely stored away in the unconscious mind to mitigate certain experiences or unwanted emotions.

Repressed memory presents a challenging subject for study due to its intricate diagnosis and connection to past trauma. Patients with suppressed memories may be able to recall them with the assistance of a therapist.

However, not all therapists guide their patients accurately, sometimes leading them to fabricate false memories rather than retrieving genuine suppressed ones, potentially resulting in misdiagnosis. It's crucial for therapists to approach this delicately, guiding patients to uncover any inaccessible memories rather than imposing suggestive scenarios.

An article by Joshua Kendall, published in April 2021 in Scientific American magazine titled "Forgotten Memories of Traumatic Events Get Some Backing from Brain-Imaging Studies: A new wave of research seeks neurological signatures for a type of amnesia," delves into repressed memories and addresses the stigma surrounding their reliability, scientifically termed dissociative amnesia.

Kendall presents two contrasting perspectives on repressed memories: one supporting their existence based on clinical evidence and the other positing that therapists or investigators may inadvertently induce patients to recall non-existent memories through misleading questioning. This debate often pits hardcore scientists advocating for the false-memory viewpoint against therapists in clinical practice advocating for the delayed-memory stance.

Researchers and clinicians studying dissociative amnesia assert that there is substantial evidence linking childhood trauma to repressed memory, considering it one of the diagnoses for PTSD (post-traumatic stress disorder).

According to Kendall, a recent paper employs magnetic resonance imaging (MRI) to examine amnesia and various other dissociative experiences often associated with severe child abuse, such as feelings of unreality and depersonalization.

On the other hand, another group argues that repressed memories are actually "false memories," basing their claims solely on observations and case studies. Approximately two decades ago, Dr. Chu conducted a study involving several women who recalled "forgotten" memories of past abuse.

However, proponents of the false-memory theory countered Chu's claims, warning that the use of leading questions by investigators could induce inaccurate recollections. Despite clinical trials conducted over time, researchers skeptical of the existence of repressed memories remain unconvinced by brain-imaging studies.

Henry Otgaar, a professor of legal psychology at Maastricht University in the Netherlands, has contributed to over 100 academic publications on false-memory research and frequently serves as an expert witness for defendants in abuse cases.

Otgaar maintains that "intact autobiographical memories are rarely—if ever—repressed." He argues that neurobiological studies offer evidence primarily for claims of memory loss due to dissociation, suggesting that there are alternative explanations, such as retrograde amnesia resulting from brain injury.

Both sides present their arguments and evidence, whether clinical or theoretical, with each staunchly believing in the accuracy of their research. However, the debate over traumatic memory forgetting and the controversy surrounding memory continues, particularly regarding neurobiological explanations.

In my view, suppressed memories do exist and serve as a coping mechanism for trauma, often resurfacing during attempts to heal and confront past abuse. When recalling a repressed memory, individuals may initially feel shocked and may seek validation from family members or friends who may have witnessed the event.

The outcome of confronting suppressed memories can be either negative or positive, depending on the guidance and support provided by the therapist. While I haven't personally experienced repressed memories, I have witnessed family members who have struggled with this condition. Recalling and addressing these memories with the help of a therapist has aided them in moving forward and coping with their experiences.

Confronting traumatic realities on both individual and societal levels and engaging in theoretical and clinical discussions is crucial for understanding the role of recollection in psychoanalysis and for facilitating healing and acceptance.

Characteristics of emotional repression manifest in various ways, even though individuals may not consciously recognize their repressed emotions. These signs include:

- o Struggling to identify and express feelings or appearing emotionally distant or numb.
- o Experiencing unexpected mood swings, such as being cheerful one minute and irritable or withdrawn the next.
- o Avoiding specific topics, people, or situations that may trigger suppressed emotions.
- o Seeking constant distractions, such as excessive work, hobbies, or screen time, to avoid confronting underlying emotions.
- o Experiencing strained relationships due to difficulty connecting emotionally, leading to communication breakdowns and misunderstandings.
- o Experiencing heightened stress levels as a result of internalized emotions.
- o Turning to substances (e.g., alcohol or drugs) or behavioral addictions (e.g., gambling, shopping, or sex) as coping mechanisms.
- o Experiencing frequent feelings of unease, sadness, or discomfort without being able to identify the source of these emotions.
- o Having difficulty talking about thoughts or feelings and becoming defensive or irritated when asked about them.

These characteristics of emotional repression indicate the presence of suppressed emotions that continue to influence psychological well-being and interpersonal interactions.

How Do Memories Get Suppressed?

The process of suppressing memories is complex and can happen for various reasons:

Traumatic Events: Memories of traumatic events such as abuse or accidents can indeed be overwhelming to deal with. In response to such overwhelming experiences, the mind may employ defense mechanisms such as repression to protect the individual from experiencing intense emotional distress.

Repression is a psychological defense mechanism identified by Sigmund Freud, which involves pushing threatening or disturbing thoughts, memories, or feelings into the unconscious mind. This process effectively removes these distressing memories from conscious awareness, allowing the individual to function without being constantly overwhelmed by them.

The intention behind repression is to shield the individual from the emotional pain associated with traumatic memories, at least temporarily. However, these memories often continue to exert an influence on the individual's thoughts, emotions, and behaviors, even when buried deep within the unconscious mind.

It's important to note that while repression may provide temporary relief from overwhelming emotions, unresolved trauma can have long-term effects on mental health and well-being. Suppressed memories may resurface unexpectedly, triggered by certain stimuli or events, leading to distressing symptoms such as flashbacks, nightmares, and intrusive thoughts.

Therapeutic approaches such as trauma-focused therapy aim to help individuals safely process and integrate traumatic memories into their conscious awareness. By creating a supportive and validating environment, therapists can assist clients in gradually confronting and making sense of their traumatic experiences, leading to healing and psychological growth.

Overall, the phenomenon of repressed memories underscores the complexity of human psychology and the profound impact that traumatic events can have on memory and emotional well-being. Recognizing and addressing these hidden memories is an essential step towards healing and recovery for individuals who have experienced trauma.

Childhood Amnesia: Childhood amnesia refers to the phenomenon where adults have limited recollection of events that occurred during early childhood, typically before the age of around three to five years old.

Several factors contribute to childhood amnesia, including the immaturity of the brain during early development, the ongoing process of neural pruning, and the lack of language skills necessary for encoding and retrieving memories. During infancy and early childhood, the brain undergoes rapid growth and development, with significant changes occurring in the structures responsible for memory formation and storage.

Moreover, the development of autobiographical memory—the ability to recall specific events and experiences from one's own life—requires the integration of various cognitive and linguistic skills that may not fully emerge until later in childhood. Without the necessary cognitive and linguistic abilities, young children may struggle to encode and retain detailed memories of past events.

Additionally, research suggests that early memories may be more susceptible to forgetting or distortion over time, as they are often based on fleeting sensory impressions and may lack the contextual details necessary for long-term retention. As a result, many childhood memories may gradually fade or become fragmented as individuals grow older.

While the exact mechanisms underlying childhood amnesia are still not fully understood, it is a widely recognized phenomenon that highlights the complex interplay between brain development, memory processes, and personal identity. Despite the limitations of early childhood memory, researchers continue to explore ways to better understand the factors that influence memory formation and retention across the lifespan.

Self-Defense: That's a common perspective on the function of suppressed memories – that they serve as a form of mental self-defense mechanism. The idea is that when individuals experience traumatic events or overwhelming emotions, their minds may repress or suppress these memories as a means of protecting them from the associated distress.

In this view, suppressed memories remain hidden in the unconscious mind until the individual's psyche deems them safe to confront. The belief is that the mind may withhold these memories until the individual has developed the necessary psychological resources and coping mechanisms to process and integrate them.

This concept aligns with theories of trauma and coping mechanisms within psychology. Traumatic events can be so overwhelming that they exceed the individual's capacity to cope effectively in the moment. In response, the mind may employ defense mechanisms such as repression to shield the individual from the full impact of the trauma.

As individuals undergo personal growth, therapy, or other forms of healing, they may gradually become better equipped to confront and process suppressed memories.

Therapeutic approaches such as trauma-focused therapy aim to create a safe and supportive environment for individuals to explore and make sense of their traumatic experiences at their own pace.

However, it's important to note that the concept of suppressed memories remains controversial in some areas of psychology, particularly regarding the accuracy and reliability of memories that resurface after being suppressed for extended periods. Some researchers argue that memories retrieved under certain conditions, such as during therapy or hypnosis, may be influenced by suggestion or other factors, potentially leading to the creation of false memories.

Overall, while the idea of suppressed memories as a form of self-defense mechanism is widely accepted in some therapeutic contexts, ongoing research is needed to better understand the complexities of memory repression and its implications for psychological well-being.

Repressed desires can stem from unfulfilled wishes and lust that conflict with societal norms, personal values or biblical teachings. For instance, individuals raised in religious households knowing that homosexuality is a sin may struggle with same-sex desires as they choose to live based upon truth.

Fearful phobias may also arise from repressed memories or experiences. When the root causes of phobias are unconsciously repressed, individuals may exhibit exaggerated reactions to specific triggers. For example, someone might fear large bodies of water without realizing that the fear originated from a near-drowning experience in childhood.

Moreover, repressed memories contributing to a negative self-image can be buried to uphold a more positive self-perception. While this mechanism protects self-esteem in the short term, it may impede personal growth in the long run.

How Long Do Suppressed Memories Last?

It's fascinating how some people can live their whole lives without ever confronting suppressed memories while others eventually find themselves facing these memories head-on. The duration of suppressed memories varies from person to person, depending on several factors:

Psychological Resilience: Some folks have strong mental resilience and coping mechanisms that allow them to function well despite suppressed memories.

Trigger Events: Suppressed memories can resurface due to certain triggers, like therapy, stress, or encountering situations similar to the suppressed memories. These triggers can bring up the memories and cause emotional distress.

Support System: A good support network can make a world of difference. Friends, family, or therapists who understand and provide guidance can help individuals navigate the challenges that come with resurfacing memories.

The Weight of and the Processing of Negative Memories

With memories being the threads that weave the fabric of our lives, a quilt of joy and sorrow. Positive memories uplift our spirits and fuel our hope, negative memories can cast a long, dark shadow over our hearts.

They can dim the light of hope and faith—the bedrock on which we build our lives and fulfill our God-given potential. In this journey of self-discovery, we will explore the realm of negative memories, drawing wisdom from both human experience and the timeless teachings of the Bible. Together, we will understand their profound impact on our emotional, mental, and physical well-being.

I intentionally use knots to represent negative memories, similarly they are stubborn and difficult to unleash. Born from experiences of trauma, loss, or emotional pain, these knots have the power to linger, casting a shadow on our daily existence. They manifest as persistent thoughts, intrusive images, or haunting emotions, disrupting our inner peace.

"Just as a knot can tangle a thread, negative memories can entangle our hearts."

The Importance of Reflection

Reflective practices are a profound way of engaging with our thoughts and experiences, allowing us to delve deep into our subconscious to understand how past events shape our current behaviors and reactions. For those who may quickly escalate to anger, are overly critical of themselves, or exhibit codependency, these patterns often have roots in past experiences or memories that may seem neutral or insignificant at first glance.

How thoroughly do you understand yourself? Have you ever contemplated the reasons behind your actions? Self-reflection is a valuable skill that facilitates a deeper comprehension of oneself.

According to Angeleena Francis, LMHC, who serves as the executive director for AMFM Healthcare, self-reflection entails being present with oneself and purposefully directing attention inward to analyze thoughts, emotions, behaviors, and motivations.

Kristin Wilson, MA, LPC, CCTP, RYT, the chief experience officer for Newport Healthcare, emphasizes that actively engaging in self-reflection can enhance understanding of one's identity, core values, and the underlying drivers behind thoughts and behaviors.

Self-reflection holds significant importance due to its role in shaping self-concept and fostering personal development.

Developing Self-Concept: Self-reflection is crucial in shaping one's self-concept, which forms a fundamental aspect of one's identity. This concept encompasses thoughts about individual traits, abilities, beliefs, values, roles, and relationships. It profoundly influences mood, judgment, and behavioral patterns.

Engaging in introspection allows individuals to deepen their self-awareness and adapt to personal changes over time. It facilitates a continuous process of self-discovery and understanding, strengthening the self-concept as individuals evolve.

Facilitating Self-Development: Self-reflection is instrumental in fostering self-development, serving as a prerequisite skill for personal growth. By evaluating strengths and weaknesses and discerning successes and failures, individuals can identify areas for improvement and advancement.

For instance, consider a scenario where a presentation at school or work falls short of expectations despite considerable effort. Through self-reflection, individuals may recognize the lack of practice in delivering the presentation as a contributing factor. Acknowledging such insights enables corrective actions, such as practicing presentations beforehand, leading to enhanced performance in similar situations.

Similarly, following a breakup, rather than attributing all blame to the partner, self-reflection enables individuals to introspect on their own behaviors that may have contributed to the relationship's dissolution. This awareness facilitates personal growth and enhances future relationship dynamics.

Without the practice of self-reflection, individuals risk perpetuating unproductive patterns and encountering recurring challenges. Embracing introspection empowers individuals to proactively address shortcomings, foster personal growth, and navigate life's complexities more effectively.

The benefits of self-reflection, as outlined by experts, encompass various aspects of personal growth and well-being:

Increased Self-Awareness: Dedicating time to self-reflection fosters heightened self-awareness, a fundamental element of emotional intelligence. This awareness enables individuals to recognize and comprehend their emotions, as well as comprehend how these emotions influence their thoughts and behaviors.

Enhanced Sense of Control: Self-reflection is about practicing mindfulness and embracing present-moment awareness. This practice promotes a greater sense of grounding and self-control, empowering individuals to navigate their experiences more effectively.

Improved Communication Skills: Self-reflection contributes to refining communication abilities, thus benefiting interpersonal relationships. By gaining insight into one's emotions, individuals can articulate themselves clearly, authentically, and empathetically.

Alignment with Core Values: Self-reflection facilitates a deeper understanding of personal beliefs and motivations. This understanding ensures that individuals' words and actions align more closely with their core values, reducing cognitive dissonance—the discomfort stemming from inconsistencies between behavior and values.

Enhanced Decision-Making Abilities: Self-reflection aids in making informed decisions. By gaining a better understanding of one, individuals can evaluate available options with clarity, ultimately making decisions that resonate more closely with their personal needs and values.

Increased Accountability: Self-reflection cultivates a sense of personal accountability. By assessing their actions and acknowledging personal responsibility, individuals become more accountable for their goals and aspirations.

In summary, self-reflection offers multifaceted benefits, ranging from heightened self-awareness and improved communication skills to enhanced decision-making abilities and increased accountability. These benefits collectively contribute to personal growth and fulfillment.

Addressing discomfort in self-reflection can be challenging, but valuable strategies exist for managing these feelings effectively. Firstly, preparing mentally is crucial, acknowledging that confronting difficult emotions is part of the process. Creating a safe space within oneself is essential, where self-criticism is replaced with observation and acceptance.

Reflective practice extends beyond mere activities, encompassing a mindset of continual adaptation through reflection. Recognizing the diverse paths to reflection, individuals can embrace a reflective mindset to navigate challenges and foster personal growth effectively.

Incorporating Graham Cooke's teachings on the importance of reflection, we learn that reflection is not just about recalling a memory; it's about allowing the Holy Spirit to provide insight into the lessons these memories hold. It's a means of receiving God's wisdom to transform our thoughts and reactions. As Cooke might suggest, reflection is an active and intentional practice where we engage with our experiences in the presence of God to gain new perspectives.

Let's Have a Look at His Teachings:

Graham Cooke's teachings on self-reflection offer valuable insights into the spiritual practice of introspection and its significance in personal growth and alignment with God's purposes. Let's delve into each key point in detail:

1. Intentional introspection: Cooke advocates for individuals to intentionally carve out time for self-reflection. This deliberate practice involves setting aside moments in one's routine to delve into one's thoughts, emotions, and actions in the context of their relationship with God. By prioritizing introspection, individuals can cultivate a deeper understanding of themselves and their spiritual journey.

2. Honest assessment: Central to Cooke's teachings is the principle of honesty and vulnerability in self-reflection. Rather than shying away from uncomfortable truths or masking weaknesses, Cooke encourages individuals to honestly assess themselves. This entails acknowledging both strengths and weaknesses, fears and desires, without judgment or condemnation. By embracing authenticity in self-assessment, individuals lay the foundation for genuine growth and transformation.

3. Alignment with God's truth: Cooke emphasizes the importance of aligning one's self-perception with God's truth and perspective. This involves discerning and rejecting negative or false beliefs about oneself and embracing the identity and purpose that God has ordained for each individual. By anchoring self-reflection in God's truth, individuals

can transcend self-limiting beliefs and embrace their true identity as beloved children of God.

4. Transformation through reflection: According to Cooke, genuine self-reflection has the power to catalyze transformation and spiritual growth. By inviting God to illuminate areas of weakness or areas in need of change, individuals open themselves up to profound personal development. Through reflection, individuals can identify patterns, overcome obstacles, and cultivate virtues such as humility, patience, and resilience. Ultimately, self-reflection becomes a catalyst for deeper intimacy with God and alignment with His purposes.

5. Practical application: Cooke provides practical tools and exercises to facilitate meaningful self-reflection. These include practices such as journaling, prayer, and meditation on Scripture. By engaging in these disciplines, individuals can deepen their self-awareness, enhance their spiritual discernment, and cultivate a more intimate relationship with God. These practical applications serve as vehicles for translating introspective insights into tangible actions and transformative growth.

In summary, Graham Cooke's teachings on self-reflection underscore the transformative power of introspection in spiritual growth and alignment with God's purposes. By embracing intentional introspection, practicing honesty and vulnerability, aligning with God's truth, and applying practical tools for reflection, individuals can embark on a journey of personal transformation and deepen their walk with God.

Biblical Foundation for Reflection:

The biblical foundation for reflection is deeply rooted in various passages throughout the Bible that encourage introspection, self-examination, and alignment with God's truth. Here's a summary of some key biblical principles that support the practice of reflection:

1. Psalm 139:23-24: This passage calls for introspection and invites God to search one's heart and thoughts, revealing any wickedness or hurtful ways within. It emphasizes the importance of self-examination and openness to God's guidance in the process.

2. Proverbs 27:19: The proverb compares the reflection of one's face in water to the reflection of one's heart. It highlights the significance of introspection in gaining insight into one's innermost thoughts, emotions, and motivations.

3. 2 Corinthians 13:5: Paul urges believers to examine themselves to see whether they are living in the faith and to test themselves. This verse underscores the importance of self-

examination in assessing one's spiritual condition and ensuring alignment with God's truth.

4. Romans 12:2: Paul encourages believers to renew their minds and not conform to the patterns of this world. This verse emphasizes the transformative power of reflection and the importance of aligning one's thoughts and beliefs with God's truth for spiritual growth and renewal.

5. James 1:23-25: James compares reflection on the word of God to looking into a mirror. He emphasizes the importance of not only hearing God's word but also applying it to one's life. This passage underscores the transformative potential of reflection on Scripture in shaping one's character and behavior.

6. Lamentations 3:40: The prophet Jeremiah calls for self-examination and repentance, urging individuals to examine their ways and turn back to the Lord. This verse highlights the role of reflection in recognizing areas of sin or disobedience and seeking reconciliation with God.

7. Philippians 4:8: Paul encourages believers to consider whatever is true, noble, right, pure, lovely, and admirable. This verse emphasizes the importance of intentional reflection on positive and uplifting thoughts, aligning one's mind with God's values and principles.

Overall, the biblical foundation for reflection underscores the importance of introspection, self-examination, and alignment with God's truth as essential components of spiritual growth, renewal, and alignment with God's purposes. These principles provide a solid framework for individuals seeking to cultivate a deeper relationship with God and live according to His will.

Applying Reflection to Neutral Memories:

Reflecting on neutral memories, even those that may seem insignificant at first glance, can indeed reveal valuable insights for spiritual and personal growth. Here's how applying reflection to neutral memories can uncover hidden treasures:

1. Patterns of Behavior: Through introspection, you can discern how seemingly mundane events have influenced your responses and behaviors. By examining these patterns, you may uncover recurring reactions or habits that have been shaping your life. Identifying these patterns allows you to evaluate whether they align with your values and desired direction. Once recognized, you can intentionally work towards altering these patterns to foster personal growth and alignment with God's will.

2. Areas for Improvement: Neutral memories can serve as a mirror reflecting behaviors that may not align with your values or the teachings of Scripture. By reflecting on these moments, you can identify areas for improvement and growth in your character and conduct. This process involves acknowledging behaviors or attitudes that may need adjustment and making conscious efforts to align them with God's word. Through prayer, self-reflection, and seeking guidance from trusted mentors or spiritual advisors, you can embark on a journey of continuous improvement and transformation.

3. Appreciation for Life: Even in the midst of seemingly ordinary moments, reflection can lead to a deeper appreciation for life and a heightened awareness of God's presence. By intentionally reflecting on neutral memories, you can cultivate a spirit of gratitude and find joy in the simple pleasures of everyday life. As the apostle Paul writes in Philippians 4:11, learning to be content in 'whatever state' you are in involves recognizing and appreciating the blessings and beauty that surround you, regardless of circumstances. Through reflection, you can develop a perspective of gratitude and contentment that transcends external circumstances and fosters spiritual growth.

In summary, applying reflection to neutral memories can uncover valuable insights into patterns of behavior, areas for improvement, and appreciation for life's blessings. By engaging in intentional introspection, you can harness the transformative power of reflection to cultivate personal and spiritual growth, aligning your life more closely with God's purposes and teachings.

Incorporating Graham Cooke's Lessons:

Graham Cooke talks about leveraging reflection to engage in conversation with God, where we can be taught, corrected, and encouraged. He suggests using reflection as a strategic tool to receive wisdom and clarity, enabling us to rise above our circumstances and enter into a place of peace and rest in God's plans for our lives.

By revisiting our memories with intentionality and seeking the Holy Spirit's guidance, we can interpret our past and present experiences through God's lens, which is a powerful catalyst for growth and change. Through this practice, we learn to see ourselves as God sees us, leading to a life transformed by His wisdom and grace.

In conclusion, in our quest to celebrate life's extraordinary events, let us not forget the significance of neutral memories. They are the underappreciated moments that make up the majority of our lives. Through repetition and seeming uneventfulness, they provide structure, stability, and a sense of balance.

From both a psychological and biblical perspective, neutral memories have unique importance. As we navigate the quilt of our lives, let us remember that every stitch, whether vibrant or neutral, plays a vital role in shaping who we are. In embracing neutral memories, we may find a deeper appreciation for the beauty of life's simple moments and the lessons they hold for us.

As we journey through life, our inherent potential often remains dormant, entangled in the knots of unresolved emotions and memories. It is my firm belief that these knots—these unresolved issues—are what hinder the brilliance of our potential from truly shining through. Throughout my over twenty years of ministry, I have observed that the key to unlocking and reclaiming one's potential often lies in addressing these very knots.

Insights from Psychological Theories

In the forthcoming chapter, we will delve into a range of psychological insights that have shaped our understanding of human behavior. It is important to note that while I do not align with all the philosophies and methodologies presented by these figures, I believe that their contributions have significant merit in understanding and addressing the complex nature of human behavior and mental health.

The theories and studies of eminent figures like B.F. Skinner and Ivan Pavlov have laid down crucial groundwork in the domain of behaviorism. Skinner's investigations into operant conditioning illustrate how behavior is molded by the consequences it faces. This understanding is pivotal in deciphering how negative memories might shape our present behavior through learned responses. Similarly, Pavlov's research on classical conditioning sheds light on how certain stimuli can elicit automatic responses, especially those tied to adverse experiences.

While these frameworks provide valuable insights into certain aspects of human psychology, they might not fully capture the entirety of the human experience. Human psychology is intricate and influenced by a multitude of factors, including emotion, cognition, spirituality, and social dynamics.

Moreover, the repercussions of unresolved negative memories on well-being are extensively discussed in psychological circles, often associated with mental health challenges like anxiety, depression, and PTSD. Therapeutic interventions, drawing from various psychological paradigms, endeavor to tackle these issues and facilitate emotional and psychological healing.

As we delve into the insights offered by these psychological theories, it's imperative to apply them judiciously, supplementing them with holistic approaches to foster a more comprehensive understanding of human behavior and emotional well-being. It's crucial to approach these theories with open-mindedness and discernment, acknowledging that each presents valuable tools for unraveling the complexities of the human mind.

"At the heart of healing lies the courage to confront our inner world, armed with the wisdom from diverse disciplines, towards a journey of transformation and renewal."

The following are light insights from psychologists, making their wisdom accessible to all.

B.F. Skinner (1904-1990):

Skinner's insights remind us that negative memories can influence our behavior through conditioning. By recognizing and addressing these conditioned responses, we can regain control over our lives.

Ivan Pavlov (1849-1936):

Pavlov's classical conditioning teaches us how negative memories can trigger automatic responses. Understanding this empowers us to recondition our reactions to painful triggers.

The Impact on Well-Being

Unresolved negative memories can have a profound impact on mental health, often manifesting in conditions such as anxiety, depression, and post-traumatic stress disorder (PTSD). These memories can linger in the subconscious, exerting influence over thoughts, emotions, and behaviors, even if the individual is unaware of them. Here's how these conditions can be affected:

Anxiety: Unresolved negative memories can contribute to the development or exacerbation of anxiety disorders. Traumatic experiences or persistent negative thoughts can create a sense of impending danger or fear, leading to chronic worry, nervousness, and physical symptoms such as rapid heartbeat, sweating, and muscle tension.

Depression: Negative memories, particularly those associated with feelings of guilt, shame, or hopelessness, can fuel depressive symptoms. When unresolved, these memories may contribute to a persistent low mood, loss of interest in activities, changes in appetite or sleep patterns, and feelings of worthlessness or despair.

PTSD: In cases where negative memories are linked to traumatic events, individuals may develop PTSD. Flashbacks, nightmares, intrusive thoughts, and hyperarousal are common symptoms experienced by those with PTSD. The unresolved nature of these memories can lead to avoidance behaviors, emotional numbness, and difficulties in functioning in daily life.

Therapeutic interventions play a crucial role in addressing unresolved negative memories and promoting emotional and psychological healing. Here are some approaches commonly used in therapy:

Cognitive Behavioral Therapy (CBT): CBT helps individuals identify and challenge negative thought patterns and beliefs associated with their memories. By reframing these thoughts and developing coping strategies, individuals can reduce the impact of negative memories on their mental health.

Eye Movement Desensitization and Reprocessing (EMDR): EMDR is particularly effective in treating PTSD and other trauma-related disorders. This therapy involves guided eye movements or other forms of bilateral stimulation while recalling traumatic memories, facilitating the processing and resolution of these memories.

Exposure Therapy: Exposure therapy gradually exposes individuals to feared or avoided situations, memories, or stimuli in a safe and controlled environment. Over time, this exposure helps desensitize individuals to their negative memories and reduces associated anxiety or distress.

Mindfulness-Based Therapies: Practices such as mindfulness meditation can help individuals develop awareness of their thoughts and emotions without judgment. By cultivating mindfulness, individuals can learn to observe and accept their negative memories without becoming overwhelmed by them.

Psychodynamic Therapy: Psychodynamic therapy explores the unconscious processes underlying an individual's thoughts, feelings, and behaviors, including those related to unresolved negative memories. Through exploration and interpretation, individuals can gain insight into the origins of their difficulties and work towards resolution.

By addressing unresolved negative memories through these therapeutic interventions, individuals can begin to heal emotionally and psychologically, reducing the impact of these memories on their mental health and overall well-being. It's essential for individuals to seek support from qualified mental health professionals who can provide personalized treatment tailored to their specific needs and circumstances.

"As we address the knots within our hearts, we untangle the threads of our well-being."

Understanding the Knots That Bind Us

Psychologists like Abraham Maslow and Erik Erikson have laid out frameworks that help us understand our complex needs and development stages. For instance, Maslow's hierarchy of needs, teaches us that until our basic needs are met, we cannot ascend to the peak of self-actualization, where our true potential lies. Similarly, Erikson's stages of psychosocial development underscore the impact of our early experiences on our growth. Both theories implicitly acknowledge that unresolved issues can stall our journey toward self-fulfillment.

The Impact of Memories on Surfacing Your Brilliance

The analogy of negative memories as knots in a tapestry beautifully captures the way these experiences can obscure our perception of ourselves and hinder our personal growth. Just as knots disrupt the smooth flow of a tapestry's pattern, negative memories can distort our self-image and prevent us from recognizing our true potential.

Confronting these memories is indeed a vital step in the healing process. By facing them head-on, we can begin the untangling the knots that have formed within us. This journey requires patience, as untangling knots can be intricate and time-consuming. It demands persistence, as progress may be slow and setbacks inevitable. However, through perseverance and determination, we can gradually unravel these knots and restore clarity to our self-perception.

Moreover, divine intervention underscores the profound and often spiritual nature of the healing process. For many, finding strength and guidance from a God, the higher power, can provide solace and direction during times of struggle. Whether through prayer, meditation, or seeking support from spiritual communities, tapping into God, the source of divine intervention can offer comfort and hope as we navigate the challenges of confronting our negative memories.

Ultimately, by embracing the process of untangling our negative memories, we can uncover the truth of who we are and reclaim our innate capacity to thrive. Like a tapestry restored to its original beauty, we emerge from this journey stronger, wiser, and more resilient, ready to embrace the fullness of our potential.

Biblical Guidance and Professional Support

When considering the healing journey, especially as it relates to the knots of negative memories and the entanglements of our past, the Bible stands as the ultimate authority for many believers. Its antiquity and the enduring nature of its wisdom offer a testament to its spiritual authority and relevance across millennia. It is not merely the age of the scriptures that grants them this authority but the consistent testimony of transformed lives throughout history.

The Bible, composed over centuries, has been the bedrock of faith for countless individuals. It has withstood the scrutiny of time, maintaining its place as a spiritual compass and a source of hope. Its longevity speaks to its ability to resonate with the human experience, offering guidance that transcends cultural and historical boundaries.

Personal Experiences with the Word of God

Personal testimonies bolster the authority of the Bible. Individuals across generations have encountered its verses and found solace, guidance, and transformative power within them. My journey with the Word of God has solidified my belief in its supreme authority. Through its teachings, I have experienced comfort in times of distress, wisdom in moments of uncertainty, and correction when I've strayed. This personal relationship with the scriptures underlines their potency and relevance.

Biblical Guidance on the Healing Journey

The Bible offers a comprehensive framework for comprehending and navigating the intricacies of human emotions and the path to healing. Isaiah 41:10 reassures us of God's presence and support in our journey: "The Lord is with you, strengthening and upholding your heart." This promise serves as a steadfast foundation as we confront the challenges of healing from negative memories.

While various psychological approaches provide insights into the human mind and behavior, their effectiveness is often heightened when they align with the biblical narrative. The Bible grants us a holistic understanding of human nature, encompassing the spiritual dimensions of our experiences. When psychology harmonizes with scriptural principles, it becomes a valuable tool in the healing process.

In the biblical context, two distinct Greek words shed light on the concept of healing: "Iaomai" and "Therapeuo."

Iaomai: This term is predominantly associated with physical healing. It signifies the act of restoring health to the body, often in response to physical ailments or disabilities. We find numerous instances of Jesus performing "Iaomai" healings in the New Testament, such as curing the blind, the lame, and those suffering from various diseases.

Therapeuo: In contrast, "Therapeuo" encompasses a broader spectrum of healing, focusing not only on physical but also on emotional, mental, and spiritual well-being. It implies a more holistic approach to healing, addressing the entirety of a person's being. This type of healing is less concerned with physical ailments and more centered on the restoration of one's inner self, their emotions, and their overall state of well-being.

It's important to note that while many examples of healing in the Bible are "Iaomai" in nature, this book leans more towards the "Therapeuo" approach. It acknowledges that healing extends beyond the physical realm and delves into our lives' emotional and spiritual dimensions. The healing journey it explores encompasses the mending of emotional wounds, the liberation from oppressive thoughts, and the restoration of inner peace.

As we navigate the complexities of healing from negative memories, we draw inspiration from the Bible's rich healing narratives, recognizing that our journey towards wholeness encompasses not only physical restoration but also the restoration of our hearts, minds, and spirits. The Bible offers a framework for understanding and navigating the complexities of human emotion and the process of healing. In Isaiah 41:10, we are reminded, "The Lord is with you, strengthening and upholding your heart," assuring us of God's presence and support.

This promise provides a solid foundation upon which we can stand as we face the challenges of healing from negative memories. While various psychological approaches offer insights into the human mind and behavior, they are most effective for many when they align with the biblical narrative. The Bible provides a holistic understanding of human nature, which includes the spiritual dimensions of our experiences. When psychology is in harmony with scriptural principles, it can be a valuable tool in the healing process.

Seeking Professional Guidance

The Bible also encourages wisdom in seeking counsel. Proverbs 11:14 states, "Where there is no guidance, a people fall, but in an abundance of counselors there is safety." Therefore, while the Bible is the ultimate authority, there is merit in seeking professional guidance, especially from those who respect the transformative power of the Word of God and integrate it into their practice.

In conclusion, healing from negative memories requires a multifaceted approach. The Bible remains the ultimate guide, offering not only principles for living but also the promise of God's direct intervention in our healing process. My experiences with the

Word of God affirm its role as the highest authority, providing a bedrock of truth and wisdom upon which we can build a journey towards wholeness. It is in integrating biblical truth with other forms of wisdom, including the insights of psychology, that we find a comprehensive path to well-being.

Shifting to a Strategic and Prayerful Approach

Now that we have equipped ourselves with knowledge about these knots, we must strategically shift our focus to prayerfully working on them. This is where faith intersects with practice. In the Bible, we find numerous instances where prayer led to breakthroughs and healing. It is through this spiritual discipline that we can ask for and receive the wisdom and strength to address the complex entanglements within our lives.

Reclaiming Your Potential

Healing is akin to unlocking a door to our true potential. As we heal, we rediscover parts of ourselves that were lost or subdued. We begin to see our past with a clearer vision, not just as a series of events that happened to us but as a rich tapestry that has shaped us into who we are meant to be. In healing, we unlock not just our potential for personal satisfaction but also our capacity to contribute meaningfully to the world around us.

Our journey of healing from these knots is much like a quilt being carefully restored. A quilt is not defined by its frayed edges or tangled threads, and similarly, our lives are more than our negative memories. With the knowledge we have gained and the divine guidance we seek, we can begin to address these burdens, reclaiming our emotional, mental, and spiritual well-being.

With a hopeful heart, we embrace this transformative journey, equipped with the insights from psychology, the unchanging wisdom of the Bible, and the lessons learned from our own experiences. Together, these tools enable us to work through our knots, paving the way for a future where our potential is not just a possibility but a reality.

"In embracing the power of positive memories and addressing the burden of negative memories, we cultivate a brighter future. We stand on the threshold of a journey of healing, hope, and rediscovery—a journey toward a heart made whole once more."

"Dear Reader,

Embarking on the journey to unravel the knots of negative memories can be a challenging and deeply emotional endeavor. It may stir up long-buried feelings, memories, and experiences that are painful to confront. However, if you are drawn to this book, I personally believe there is a divine anointing for healing that will meet you on this path.

In this journey, we seek healing guided by faith, trust, and divine wisdom. It is an intimate exploration that requires a haven and a profound connection with the Holy Spirit. Along the way, you will also discover the invaluable support of a compassionate counselor or therapist who can walk beside you during this transformative experience.

Together, let us explore the process of untangling the knots of negative memories, drawing strength from our faith and the divine presence. In the words that follow, you will find guidance, encouragement, and the light of faith to help you navigate the sometimes-tumultuous waters of memory healing.

May the anointing for healing within these pages meet you where you are, and may you find the peace, strength, and wholeness you seek.

With faith and compassion,

Let's Begin

In the journey to untangle the knots of negative memories, we embark on a path of healing guided by faith, trust, and divine wisdom. This process is an intimate and emotional one, necessitating a safe haven and a profound connection with the Holy Spirit. Additionally, the presence of a compassionate counselor or therapist can provide essential support throughout this transformative journey.

Voluntary Memory Reflection and the Holy Spirit's Role

As you set out on this personal odyssey, it's vital to choose a safe and peaceful environment where you can find solace. This might be a quiet room, a serene garden, or any place that encourages self-reflection without external distractions. Creating this safe space is the first step in allowing your heart and mind to explore the depths of your memories.

Invoking the Holy Spirit:

The Bible imparts the understanding that the Holy Spirit is not an impersonal force but a distinct person. Jesus consistently referred to the Holy Spirit as "He," emphasizing its personhood rather than using the impersonal pronoun "it." In passages like John 14, 15, and 16, the language employed underscores the personal nature of the Holy Spirit.

Instances like the King James Version's use of "itself" in Romans 8:16 are recognized as mistranslations. Most contemporary translations have corrected this to "himself," aligning with the biblical portrayal of the Holy Spirit as a person with intellect, emotions, and will.

The Bible attributes the Holy Spirit's actions as indicative of a genuine person. The Spirit speaks, as seen in passages like Revelation 2:7 and Acts 13:2. Furthermore, the Spirit intercedes on behalf of believers, as articulated in Romans 8:26, testifies of the truth in John 15:26, leads individuals, as evidenced in Acts 8:29 and Romans 8:14, and even issues commands, as observed in Acts 16:6–7. Acknowledging the Holy Spirit's personhood enhances our comprehension of its multifaceted role as an active and guiding presence in our lives.

The Holy Spirit's role extends beyond guidance, as outlined in John 16:13 (RSV). It encompasses appointments, as illustrated in Acts 20:28, where the Holy Spirit designates overseers for the church. Furthermore, the Holy Spirit, being a person, is susceptible to certain interactions; one can lie to Him, as exemplified in the account of Ananias and Sapphira in Acts 5:3–4.

Moreover, the Holy Spirit can be insulted, as emphasized in Hebrews 10:29, and blasphemed, as warned in Matthew 12:31–32. The ability to experience grief is attributed to the Holy Spirit, as noted in Ephesians 4:30. These emotional responses and actions, distinctively characteristic of a person, reinforce the understanding that the Holy Spirit is not a mere impersonal force like gravity or magnetism. Instead, the Holy Spirit is a person with a rich array of attributes and a divine nature. Recognizing these aspects deepens our appreciation for the intricate and personal connection we share with the Holy Spirit in our spiritual journey.

The Bible consistently affirms that the Holy Spirit is none other than God Himself. This profound truth is evident in the divine attributes ascribed to the Holy Spirit throughout

Scripture. Examining these attributes reveals a striking alignment with the characteristics of God.

The eternal nature of the Holy Spirit is emphasized, signifying His existence throughout all time. In Hebrews 9:14, the reference to the "eternal Spirit" underscores the timeless nature of the Holy Spirit, emphasizing that there was never a point when He did not exist.

The omnipotent power of the Holy Spirit is evident in passages such as Luke 1:35, where the angel describes the Holy Spirit's role in the conception of the Son of God. This proclamation highlights the all-encompassing and potent nature of the Holy Spirit, echoing the omnipotence inherent in God.

The omnipresence of the Holy Spirit is also illuminated in Psalms 139:7, affirming His ability to be present everywhere simultaneously. This attribute aligns with the omnipresence characteristic of God, reinforcing the divine nature of the Holy Spirit.

These attributes firmly establish the Holy Spirit as not merely a force or entity but as God Himself, eternal, all-powerful, and omnipresent. This recognition deepens our understanding of the profound divine nature inherent in the Holy Spirit as revealed in the Scriptures.

The omniscience of the Holy Spirit, encompassing His all-knowing nature, is explicitly articulated in 1 Corinthians 2:10–11. The Spirit's ability to reveal the depths of God and comprehend the thoughts of God is likened to the way the spirit of a person comprehends their own thoughts, highlighting the comprehensive understanding intrinsic to the Holy Spirit.

Moreover, the Holy Spirit is unequivocally identified as God in Acts 5:3–4, emphasizing the gravity of lying to the Holy Spirit as tantamount to lying to God Himself. This declaration underscores the divine identity of the Holy Spirit and solidifies the understanding that He is an integral part of the Godhead.

The interrelation between the Lord and the Spirit is expounded in 2 Corinthians 3:18 (RSV), affirming that as individuals behold the glory of the Lord, they are transformed into His likeness by the Spirit. This connection underscores the unity within the Godhead, portraying the Holy Spirit as an essential and divine agent in the transformative process.

These scriptural passages collectively underscore the Holy Spirit's comprehensive knowledge and divine identity, further reinforcing the understanding that the Holy Spirit is not only a distinct person but an integral aspect of the triune God.

The Holy Spirit's role as the Creator is evident from the very beginning of the Bible. Genesis 1:2 (Moffatt) introduces the Spirit of God, hovering over the waters during the creation narrative. This occurrence aligns seamlessly with Genesis 1:1, which declares, "In the beginning, God created the heavens and the earth." The unity of God the Father, God the Son (as revealed in Colossians 1), and God the Holy Spirit in the act of creation is foundational.

In Paul's letter to the Colossians, the profound truth about the Lord Jesus Christ is expounded. Colossians 1:16–17 underscores that all things, both visible and invisible, were created through Him and for Him. This scriptural passage affirms the collaborative effort of God the Father, God the Son, and God the Holy Spirit in the creation of the world. It highlights the preeminence of Christ, who not only participated in creation but also sustains and holds everything together.

Recognizing and embracing these foundational truths is paramount for every Christian, both in theological understanding and practical application. Acknowledging the shared role of the triune God in creation deepens our appreciation for the interconnectedness and unity within the Godhead, shaping our perspective on the divine nature of the Holy Spirit as the Creator alongside God the Father and God the Son.

In addressing the question of the Holy Spirit's placement and potential implications of inferiority, it's crucial to recognize that the typical order of mention in the New Testament concerning the Father, the Son, and the Holy Spirit is not indicative of any hierarchy or inequality. For instance, Romans 15:30 breaks from the conventional sequence by highlighting the love of the Spirit, emphasizing the collaborative nature of the triune God.

Ephesians 4:4 further reinforces the equality among the members of the Trinity, stating that there is one body and one Spirit, emphasizing their unity in purpose and essence.

The customary order of reference to the three Persons of the Trinity is more about their distinct functions and chronological involvement rather than indicating any hierarchy. The traditional expression of praying to the Father through the Son and in the power of the Holy Spirit exemplifies this functional distinction.

Functionally, the Father initiates, the Son incarnates, dies, and rises again, while the Holy Spirit carries out His work in the present age. This order reflects the chronological unfolding of the divine plan rather than suggesting any inequality among the Persons of the Trinity.

Practically, one can invite the Holy Spirit into their sacred space, seeking his guidance and allowing the him to illuminate the sequence in which negative memories should be explored. Trusting in this spiritual connection can pave the way for healing, providing insight and understanding into the complexities of one's past.

Counselor Support:

Emotional and psychological trauma stems from highly stressful events that disrupt your sense of safety, leaving you feeling vulnerable in a threatening world. Such trauma can result in persistent emotional distress, disturbing memories, and enduring anxiety. It may also induce a sense of detachment, numbness, and an inability to trust others.

Traumatic incidents typically involve a threat to life or safety, but any situation that overwhelms you and leaves you feeling isolated can lead to trauma, even without physical harm. The determining factor isn't the objective circumstances of the event but rather your subjective emotional response. The more frightened and powerless you feel, the greater the likelihood of experiencing trauma.

Handling the aftermath of a natural disaster or human-made catastrophe poses distinct challenges, even if you weren't directly affected. Despite the slim chances of being direct victims of events like terrorist attacks, plane crashes, or mass shootings, exposure to graphic images via social media and news outlets can overwhelm your nervous system, leading to traumatic stress.

Regardless of the cause or timing of your trauma, whether it occurred recently or in the distant past, you have the capacity to initiate healing and move forward with your life.

Speak to a Licensed Therapist

Consulting with a licensed therapist or counselor who specializes in trauma and emotional recovery can be highly beneficial. Their professional knowledge and skills can provide invaluable support and guidance as you navigate through your healing process. They offer a safe and supportive environment where you can explore your emotions and memories, and their expertise can serve as a source of encouragement and solace.

In addition to seeking professional help, drawing on spiritual resources can also be comforting and empowering. As the Bible verse from Psalm 34:18 reminds us, "The Lord is close to the brokenhearted and saves those who are crushed in spirit." And from Philippians 4:13, "I can do all things through Him who strengthens me." These verses can provide reassurance and a sense of divine presence during challenging times.

Involuntary Memory Processing through Emotional Awareness

Acceptance and Letting Go

As you delve deeper into your memories, be prepared to face the emotions that have long been buried or suppressed.

What is Letting Go?

Letting go is about not letting past negative experiences impact our present or future. It's the act of freeing ourselves from the emotional weight of these experiences, recognizing that dwelling on them doesn't benefit us. Similarly, it involves easing the anxiety about the future, allowing us to be fully present in the current moment.

In simpler terms, letting go means living in the now and not letting past hurts or future uncertainties dictate our emotions. This process liberates us from emotional baggage, enabling us to stop taking things personally and fostering a more balanced and peaceful state of mind.

Comparably, adapting to new thoughts and beliefs is like changing old shoes that no longer fit. When past memories don't align with our present situation or contribute positively to our lives, it becomes essential to replace them with new perspectives. Though it might not be easy, this shift is necessary for personal growth, productivity, and happiness. Remember, happiness often stems from our ability to release the hold of the past and embrace the possibilities of the present.

Letting go can be challenging for various reasons, rooted in the complex nature of human emotions and experiences. Here are some common reasons why it's difficult to let go:

- Emotional Attachment to Negative Memories: People often become emotionally attached to bad memories because these experiences carry intense negative emotions, making it hard to release them.
- Resistance to Accepting Reality: Difficulty in letting go may stem from an unwillingness to accept the reality of a situation and the need for change.
- Impact on Priorities and Desires: Bad experiences can significantly affect a person's priorities and important desires, making it challenging to move on from the associated emotions.

- Desire for Proper Treatment: Some individuals find it hard to let go when they believe they deserve proper treatment or justice, even if it is not always realized.
- Investment of Effort: When someone has invested significant effort into a person or goal, accepting an unfavorable outcome becomes emotionally challenging.
- Betrayal in Close Relationships: Betrayal by someone close can lead to a questioning of faith in humanity and relationships, making it difficult to trust again.
- Loss of Loved Ones: Losing someone, whether expected or unexpected, can create a profound emotional impact, making it hard to let go of the memories associated with that person.
- Perceived Injustice: Feeling that life is unjust and receiving unexpected outcomes can lead to resistance in accepting and letting go of the situation.
- Self-Inflicted Harm: Instances where individuals have inadvertently caused harm to their own lives or others due to carelessness can result in guilt and difficulty in letting go.

Understanding these reasons can be a first step towards developing coping mechanisms and strategies to navigate the process of letting go and moving forward in a healthier way.

Moreover this phase requires heightened emotional awareness and self-compassion.

Emotional Awareness:

In the journey of memory healing, the terrain of emotions can be both large, often resembling a ball of feelings that have long been concealed. It's important to recognize that identifying these emotions may prove challenging. You may fear that by delving into these deep waters, you'll lose control. The uncertainty can be unsettling, but rest assured, you will be okay.

When you venture into the realm of emotional awareness, it may feel as though you are stepping into uncharted territory. Emotions you've buried may rise to the surface like a tempestuous sea. It's natural to be apprehensive when faced with this surge of feelings, but remember that it is a necessary part of the healing process. Just as a storm clears the air, allowing for fresh, rejuvenating breaths, the release of these emotions can cleanse your soul. This is the testimony of many individuals that I have had the opportunity to work with.

Emotional awareness operates on a basic, biological level, primarily involving the intricate workings of our brain, particularly the limbic system. Here's a simplified breakdown of how emotional awareness functions:

Initial Response: When we encounter an event, our senses relay information to the amygdala, a key component of the brain responsible for processing emotions. This prompts an initial emotional response, often rapid and instinctive.

Emotion Identification: The prefrontal cortex, a region of the brain associated with decision-making and behavior control, comes into play. It assists in identifying and labeling the specific emotions we are experiencing. This step allows us to consciously recognize and understand our emotional state.

Emotion Management: Through ongoing awareness and practice, we develop the ability to manage our reactions to these emotions. This entails learning to regulate and respond to our feelings in a more intentional and constructive manner. Activities and exercises aimed at enhancing emotional awareness can contribute to improved emotion management skills.

In essence, emotional awareness involves a dynamic interplay between the initial, instinctive emotional response and the conscious identification and management of these emotions. This skill can be honed over time through intentional efforts, leading to greater self-understanding and more effective emotional regulation.

The amygdala, nestled deep within the brain, is pivotal as our emotional response center. When an event unfolds, our senses swiftly communicate with the amygdala, which promptly evaluates the situation and initiates an emotional reaction.

The prefrontal cortex, on the other hand, emerges as a key player in the realm of emotional awareness. Positioned in the frontal part of the brain, this area contributes significantly to identifying and labeling our emotions. It enables us to discern whether we are feeling sadness, anger, joy, or fear, providing a conscious understanding of our emotional state.

The crux of emotional awareness lies in mastering emotional management. Recognizing our emotions empowers us to pause, reflect, and deliberately choose how we respond to a given situation. This is where practices such as emotional awareness exercises and prayer coupled with meditation come into play, fostering the development of skills that enhance our ability to manage emotional responses effectively.

It's essential to grasp the science behind emotional awareness with the understanding that the goal is not to control or suppress emotions but rather to manage our responses to them. The process involves acknowledging and comprehending our emotions, allowing us to navigate situations with greater intentionality.

The benefits of emotional awareness extend beyond self-awareness; they pave the way for healthier relationships, improved mental health, and overall well-being. By recognizing and understanding our emotions, we gain valuable insights into our reactions, responses, and behaviors, fostering increased self-understanding and self-acceptance.

Exploring emotional awareness involves practical techniques, exercises, and activities designed to enhance our understanding and management of emotions. Key techniques include mindfulness, urging us to be present and attentive to our feelings without judgment, and emotional journaling, a regular practice of recording emotions and triggers to identify patterns.

Pausing and reflecting on emerging emotions provides a deeper understanding of our emotional reactions. Emotional awareness exercises, such as the body scan, involve paying attention to sensations in different parts of the body linked to emotions. In contrast, emotional role-play helps prepare for real-life scenarios.

Consistent practice of emotion identification contributes to improved emotional literacy. Beyond formal exercises, daily activities like prayer coupled with meditation, artistic expression through painting or writing, and engaging with emotionally rich content, such as reading or watching emotional stories, seamlessly weave emotional awareness into our routines. These activities provide opportunities for growth, fostering a greater understanding of emotions and contributing to enhanced emotional well-being.

Scriptural Comfort:

"The Lord is my rock, my fortress, and my deliverer; my God is my rock, in whom I take refuge, my shield and the horn of my salvation, my stronghold." – Psalm 18:2

"When I am afraid, I put my trust in you." – Psalm 56:3

Strategies for Facing and Releasing Emotions

Embracing the Flow

As we allow ourselves to fully experience our emotions, it's essential to approach this process without judgment or fear. It may be helpful for you to take a moment and consider that emotions you experience are not adversaries and enemies trying to take you out, despite the feeling that many may experience when they hit a tipping point. Rather, they convey needs, highlight boundaries, and signal values and passions. They demand to be felt and acknowledged, and in this acknowledgment, there is release.

There can be moments when the flow of emotions feels overwhelming, threatening to flood the banks of our stability. If you feel submerged as you read, know that it's okay to pause, step back, and return when you feel more grounded. It's essential to approach this journey with self-compassion, allowing yourself the space and time needed to process each emotion.

The Cleansing Power of Emotional Release

As you navigate through these emotions, envision the river cleansing the landscape—your soul—making space for new growth and healing. This process of emotional release is not a sign of weakness but a brave step towards renewal and strength. With each release, there is a shedding of the old, a lightness that comes from letting go of what no longer serves you. I encourage you to pause for a moment and reflect on this.

Facing the Unknown with Trust

Confronting the depth and breadth of your emotions can be very overwhelming. The uncertainty of what you might find in your emotional depths could be intimidating, and the fear of losing control is not uncommon. In these moments, I encourage you to remember that you are not by yourself. The same God that has brought calm to turbulent seas throughout history is with you in this journey.

The Bible speaks of God calming the stormy seas and bringing order to chaos. In moments when the river of emotions seems wild and relentless, you can trust in this enduring promise. Trust in His presence to guide you, to steady you, and to provide safe passage through the currents. As you read on and reflect upon the emotions that rise within you, remember that this is a personal journey.

It is a path of discovery, healing, and ultimately, freedom. The river of emotions is yours to navigate, with trust in divine guidance and the understanding that this journey is a testament to your courage and your desire for a renewed heart and spirit. In this sacred space of emotional awareness, you are invited to release what has long burdened your heart.

Trust that the cleansing flow of emotions will lead you to a place of healing and wholeness. Though the journey may be challenging, it is also profoundly transformative, allowing you to emerge stronger and lighter, much like a river that has carved its path through solid rock. Embrace this process, and you will find that, in letting go, you gain more than you could ever imagine.

Scriptural Comfort:

"When you pass through the waters, I will be with you; and when you pass through the rivers, they will not sweep over you." – Isaiah 43:2

"He stilled the storm to a whisper; the waves of the sea were hushed." – Psalm 107:29

The Path of Letting Go of Shame and Guilt

In the profound journey of untangling the knots, one of the most challenging yet liberating steps is letting go of the burdens of shame and guilt. This process can be tough, as relinquishing these heavy emotions is often akin to shedding layers of pain that have clung to your soul for far too long.

However, it is essential to understand that when you are able to forgive both others and yourself, this burden becomes easier to release, and you will begin to feel a weight lifting from your heart and spirit.

It is also crucial to acknowledge that letting go can be tough. Your emotions may have become familiar, almost like old companions, despite their toxic nature. Letting go of them may initially feel uncomfortable as if you are leaving behind a part of yourself. Lean into this discomfort, for it is a sign of growth and healing.

Forgiveness is the key that unlocks the chains of shame and guilt. It is a powerful act of self-love and compassion. When you extend forgiveness to others and yourself, you set yourself free from the shackles of the past. Like shedding a heavy cloak, forgiveness allows you to step into the lightness of being, unburdened by the weight of shame and guilt.

As you begin this process, be prepared for the unfamiliar sensation of lightness that will follow. Your body and soul will need time to adjust to this newfound freedom. It may feel unsettling at first, like a ship that has cast off its anchor and is now navigating uncharted waters. Embrace this feeling, for it is a sign that you are on the path to healing and transformation.

As you embark on this journey of letting go, remember that the discomfort you may initially feel is a sign of progress. Embrace it with open arms, for it is the precursor to the profound healing and freedom that await you on the other side.

"The wound is the place where the Light enters you." – Rumi.

I encourage you to seek peace and understanding in your current moment. Acknowledge that you have grown and evolved since those negative experiences, and that you are no longer the person you once were. The following are instructions on how to present-moment focusing and exercise self-compassion.

Present-Moment Focus:

Ground yourself in the present and remind yourself that you are no longer defined by the past. The Holy Spirit will guide you to understand how your past experiences have shaped you into the person you are today. Embrace the wisdom you've gained and the strength you've developed through life's challenges.

The objective of grounding frequently involves guiding individuals back to the present moment and reality, a practice often sought by individuals grappling with persistent and overwhelming distress. Instances of stress can trigger a fight-flight-freeze response, characterized by various uncomfortable symptoms that can be daunting to endure.

Consequently, grounding serves as a means to redirect attention, fostering a focused engagement with one task or sensation at a time, thereby slowing down the overwhelming pace. In essence, it parallels the concept of self-soothing, prioritizing the calming of our bodies amidst stress or intense emotions.

In addition to shifting attention and fostering a connection with the present, grounding aids in distancing oneself from internal emotional turmoil. It allows for the mastery over one's feelings to ensure personal safety. This process, known as "healthy detachment," is particularly prevalent among individuals contending with potent emotions and traumatic memories, such as anxiety, anger, flashbacks, and nightmares.

Trauma survivors may find themselves oscillating between states of hypervigilance and emotional numbness. Grounding techniques serve to anchor individuals to the present moment, facilitating a return to bodily equilibrium, often described as homeostasis—the body's innate ability to maintain stability. Moreover, it enables individuals to strike a balance between acknowledging reality and developing strategies to cope with it effectively.

The utilization of grounding techniques is not restricted by time or place, making them versatile tools that can be employed at any moment, whether alone or in public settings. A key aspect of grounding techniques involves recognizing internal warning signals and employing specific methods to maintain focus, such as practicing diaphragmatic breathing to regulate breathing pace or engaging in sensory exercises like the 5-4-3-2-1 senses exercise to shift attention from internal to external stimuli.

Mastering grounding techniques may require time and consistent practice, but as familiarity with the skill grows, its application becomes more seamless and intuitive. With regular practice, individuals can develop the ability to seamlessly incorporate grounding techniques, even in high-stress situations. Consequently, the cultivation of grounding practices facilitates periodic regulation of the body's responses, enhancing preparedness to confront any challenges that may arise.

To employ grounding techniques effectively, one can utilize two distinct approaches: Sensory Awareness and Cognitive Awareness. Sensory awareness involves directing attention towards specific sensory aspects of the body, while cognitive awareness pertains to understanding and focusing on mental actions or processes.

However, for this week's focus, we will begin by exploring how to integrate sensory awareness to establish a connection with the present moment. When seeking to "ground" oneself, it is advantageous to prioritize connecting with the body and enhancing sensory awareness before shifting attention to cognitive processes in the brain.

Sensory awareness grounding exercise: Deep Breathing

Utilizing deep breathing, also called diaphragmatic breathing, serves as a technique to enhance oxygen supply to the brain and activate the parasympathetic nervous system, promoting a state of calmness. By employing a specific breathing technique and rhythm, deep breathing facilitates a sense of bodily connection, redirecting attention from worries and enabling control over breathing pace.

Breathing Technique: Deep Breathing

Find a comfortable seated position, ensuring your knees are bent and that your shoulders, head, and neck are relaxed. Place one hand on your chest and the other hand over your belly button. Focus your attention on your breath, allowing only the hand on your belly button to move as you inhale deeply and exhale slowly.

Monitor the hand on your chest for signs of shallow, rapid breathing indicated by upward movement. Simultaneously, observe the hand on your belly button for the deep breaths that draw air into your lungs.

Concentrate on inhaling deeply, causing the hand on your belly button to rise as the air fills your lungs. If the hand on your chest rises instead of the hand on your belly button, it suggests shallow breathing, which is less effective in promoting a calmer state of being.

Breathing Technique: Box Breathing

Box breathing, an extension of deep breathing, incorporates counting and visual cues to enhance its effectiveness. By using a finger to trace a square shape in the air or mentally visualizing it, individuals can regulate the timing and duration of inhalation, breath holding, and exhalation. This structured approach to breathing aids in maintaining a steady and calm breathing rhythm.

Focus on each side of the imaginary box separately, allowing 4 seconds for each side. During the upward movement, inhale deeply for 4 seconds, ensuring that the abdomen rises instead of the chest lifting.

- Hold your breath for 4 seconds while completing the second side of the box.
- Exhale slowly for 4 seconds as you trace the third side of the box.
- Hold your breath for 4 seconds while completing the fourth and final side of the box.
- Repeat the process from step 1, ensuring that each inhalation, exhalation, and breath hold lasts for 4 seconds.

Initially, practice this exercise for approximately 5 to 10 minutes, repeating it 3 to 4 times per day. Gradually increase the duration to 20 to 30 minutes to further solidify the technique's effectiveness. This will enable you to seamlessly incorporate the technique as a proactive strategy when feeling overwhelmed or as a means to manage distress during stressful situations.

Sensory Awareness Grounding Exercise: 5, 4, 3, 2, 1 Exercise

This exercise serves to engage your senses by encouraging you to identify and focus on your immediate surroundings. By directing attention to sensory stimuli, this exercise facilitates a heightened awareness of the present moment and encourages the utilization of bodily sensations to elicit specific sensory responses and feedback.

- Identify 5 things you can see in your current environment.
- Recognize 4 things you can feel or touch.
- Acknowledge 3 things you can hear at this moment.
- Identify 2 things you can smell presently (alternatively, recall 2 preferred scents if environmental cues are unavailable).
- Notice 1 thing you can taste (similarly, recall 1 preferred flavor or taste if immediate sensory input is lacking).

The aim of this exercise is to re-establish a connection between mind and body through sensory engagement. Our innate senses serve as reminders of our presence in the here and now, fostering a sense of safety. By engaging with the external environment through sensory exploration, we can alleviate internal overwhelm and return to a centered state of being.

In conclusion, grounding techniques provide a safe pathway to reorient ourselves to the present moment. Consistent practice of these techniques enables them to become second nature and readily available during moments of distress.

Experiment with various grounding methods and assess their effectiveness in promoting calmness and stability. The more attuned you become to your body's sensations, the greater your sense of calmness and safety, irrespective of external circumstances. By attending to sensations that evoke feelings of comfort and tranquility, you can discover a greater sense of control over your well-being.

Self-Compassion: Extend self-compassion to yourself throughout this journey. Recognize that you did the best you could with the knowledge and resources available at the time. Forgive yourself and allow the Holy Spirit to work in your heart, bringing healing and grace, just as a gentle rain nurtures the earth.

When faced with intense negative emotions triggered by certain events, it often signifies the awakening of old childhood wounds that lie dormant within us. In such moments, a doorway to our unconscious opens, beckoning us to confront and embrace ourselves in order to heal these wounds.

Our societal conditioning may encourage us to ignore this doorway, seeking solace in addictive substances or behaviors instead. However, when the pain becomes unbearable, we may find ourselves drawn to resources like this platform or the pages of a book, ready to embark on a journey towards healing and reclaiming our well-being.

All our wounds, at their core, stem from a false belief in our separation from our spiritual core. Ultimately, it is when we are able to reconnect with God, that we can see unlimited healing . Thus, the initial step in any effective healing practice involves aligning ourselves with God and his original design. This entails cultivating self-compassion, a crucial aspect of unraveling the core wounds that linger within our spirit man's core. Until we offer ourselves compassion, these wounds remain unresolved.

For lasting healing, we must acknowledge our wounds and extend love to these vulnerable parts of ourselves, beginning with self-compassion. This conscious act of self-compassion serves as a cornerstone for our journey towards permanent healing and well-being.

Demonstrating compassion for oneself involves embracing a deeply aware and non-judgmental stance towards oneself, akin to being a loyal and supportive friend. It entails a willingness to accompany oneself through moments of pain with love and understanding.

Self-compassion encompasses a myriad of qualities such as care, concern, sensitivity, warmth, unconditional love, tenderness, acceptance, mercy, kindness, and charity towards oneself. An internal softness that permeates emotional wounds with acceptance, love, and intimate understanding.

As individuals, we possess unparalleled insight into our own feelings and hurts. We intimately understand the intricacies and depths of our pain firsthand, making us uniquely qualified to extend love and compassion to these vulnerable parts of ourselves.

Self-compassion involves beholding our tender wounds without judgment, allowing ourselves to acknowledge and feel the reality of our pain without seeking to conceal it or immediately remedy it.

This level of self-love opens doors to understanding the origins of our pain. Through befriending ourselves with love and compassion, we gain awareness of the circumstances that contributed to our wounds and the negative beliefs about ourselves that arose from these experiences.

Compassion grants us the ability to perceive ourselves as Source sees us. It embodies a divine quality, providing access to the highest realms of healing and well-being. Through compassion, we intimately experience the unconditional love of Source, feeling wholly loved in every fiber of our being.

Self-compassion is vital for our psychological healing and well-being because it addresses wounds or constrictions that originate from a sense of separation from Love within our human spirits.

While receiving love and compassion from others can be beneficial in learning to open and receive, true transformative healing comes from within ourselves. At the core of every wound lies a belief that we are separate from God, from Love—a fear of the unworthiness of love that we have internalized.

Self-compassion enables us to release this belief by experiencing the absolute truth of our inherent Loveliness. Although external affirmations may temporarily uplift us, the wounded part of our psyche will continue to hold onto feelings of inadequacy until we genuinely acknowledge our worthiness from within.

Affirmations alone cannot dismantle the core belief of separateness from the Love of God; it requires the profound realization that we are infinitely loved. This realization completes a psychological loop essential for permanent healing, preventing the recurrence of painful scenarios in our lives.

By prioritizing our healing journey, we gain insights into our past actions and behaviors, understanding that they stem from pain rather than inherent "badness." This awareness paves the way for self-compassion and well-being, as we recognize that our reactions were driven by a lack of belief in our own worthiness.

Ultimately, self-compassion allows us to confront the root cause of our wounds—the belief in separation from God—and replace it with the Truth that we have always been connected to the Lorad and are inherently deserving of his Love, including our own. This shift in perception is fundamental for achieving lasting psychological healing and well-being.

In this profound journey of unraveling negative memories, maintain a strong sense of safety, trust in the divine guidance of the Holy Spirit, and lean on the support of a trusted counselor. Through voluntary memory reflection and involuntary memory processing, you can find healing and peace.

The Holy Spirit's presence and counsel will illuminate your path towards understanding and liberation from the burdens of the past, allowing you to embrace a brighter and more hopeful future guided by faith. This journey, much like a winding river, may have its twists and turns, but with faith and perseverance, you can navigate its waters and emerge stronger and more whole on the other side.

"Healing may not be so much about getting better as about letting go of everything that isn't you—all of the expectations, all of the beliefs—and becoming who you are." – Rachel Naomi Remen

Chapter 5:   The Effects of Trauma on Memory: Navigating the Shadows

In our exploration of memory healing, we are compelled to traverse the shadowed realms of traumatic experiences that persistently haunt the corridors of our minds. Trauma wields the power to profoundly shape our recollections, etching deep scars that may seem insurmountable. To journey through this challenging terrain, we must first comprehend the profound effects of trauma on memory, then employ strategies for processing these experiences, ultimately finding hope and restoration through self-compassion.

Emotional Wounds from Trauma

The Emotional Turbulence of Trauma

Trauma, much like an unrelenting storm, has the capacity to reshape our lives in ways we could never anticipate. It embodies the tempest that rages within us, leaving emotional wreckage strewn in its wake. As we delve into the pages of the book, we confront the profound impact of emotional wounds wrought by trauma and the critical imperative to understand and address them.

Defining Trauma and Emotional Wounds

Trauma stands as a complex, encompassing term, representing a wide array of experiences that overwhelm our capacity to cope effectively. Whether it manifests in the aftermath of a natural disaster, the horrors of war, the enduring scars of abuse, or the haunting memories of a car accident, trauma takes on countless forms. Regardless of its origin, trauma leaves behind deep emotional wounds that can endure for years, perhaps even a lifetime.

The ACEs Connection: Adverse Childhood Experiences (ACEs)

To gain a unique comprehension of emotional wounds from trauma, we can explore the concept of Adverse Childhood Experiences (ACEs). In recent decades, research has unveiled a compelling link between childhood trauma and the development of emotional and physical health challenges in adulthood.

ACEs encompass a wide spectrum of traumatic experiences endured during childhood, including abuse, neglect, household dysfunction, and the witnessing of violence. These experiences possess the potential to leave an enduring imprint on an individual's emotional well-being.

The connection between ACEs and my book's exploration of emotional wounds from trauma is sound. The book underscores the universality of emotional pain and the pressing need for healing, while ACEs research sheds a revealing light on specific sources of these wounds, particularly those rooted in childhood.

The emotional wreckage left behind by traumatic experiences has the potential to endure into adulthood, significantly impacting our mental, emotional, and even physical health. I particularly like to use ACEs to help illustrate to individuals how the often stubborn knots can form in our lives.

Scriptural Insights on Healing from Emotional Wounds

Turning to Scripture, we find guidance and solace for those navigating the shadowy terrain of emotional wounds.

Psalm 34:18 states, "The Lord is close to the brokenhearted and saves those who are crushed in spirit." This verse underscores the compassionate nature of God, who draws near to us in our pain, offering salvation from the depths of despair.

Additionally, Isaiah 53:4-5 reminds us of the redemptive power of Christ's sacrifice: "Surely he took up our pain and bore our suffering... by his wounds, we are healed." This powerful passage emphasizes that through Christ's suffering and sacrifice, we can find healing from our emotional wounds. It speaks to the transformative power of faith in our journey toward wholeness.

Navigating the Storm: Healing and Hope

As we continue to explore the emotional wounds from trauma within the context of the book, we delve deeper into the process of healing and the wellspring of hope that sustains us.

The Healing Journey

Healing from emotional wounds is not linear; it more closely resembles navigating through a tempestuous sea. There are moments of calm and clarity, but also times of turbulence and uncertainty. Confronting the emotional wreckage left behind by trauma requires great courage, often necessitating professional help and the support of loved ones.

Emotional healing is a deeply personal journey that requires us to confront the pain harbored within our hearts. It entails a courageous exploration of our emotions, wherein we gently tend to our wounded selves. This transformative process necessitates vulnerability and the acknowledgment of the scars that have shaped us. Through this acceptance, genuine healing can commence.

In the pursuit of emotional healing, we develop the ability to navigate our emotional landscape with compassion and resilience. We allow ourselves to fully experience our pain, shedding tears that cleanse past wounds and embracing the growth that arises from our challenges. This journey, though demanding, grants us the strength to release burdens, leading to solace and liberation as we move forward with renewed hope and emotional well-being.

The realization of the need for emotional healing often emerges during poignant moments in life, compelling us to embark on a transformative journey of self-discovery and healing. Indications that underscore the necessity for emotional healing encompass persistent, overwhelming sadness or a deep sense of emptiness that weighs heavily on our hearts. The presence of consuming anger, leading to frequent outbursts or strained relationships, serves as another poignant sign. Lingering anxiety or fear that impedes our ability to embrace peace and joy, along with repeating patterns of self-destructive behavior or reliance on unhealthy coping mechanisms, may also signal a call for emotional healing. Challenges in forming or maintaining meaningful connections with others add to the indicators, as do lingering wounds from past traumas that continue to impact our overall well-being. When these signs manifest, they gently prompt us to practice self-compassion, seek support, and approach the journey of emotional healing with courage and resilience.

Before embarking on the journey of healing, it's essential to take a moment for self-reflection and consider some important questions. These questions act as a guide, helping us gain a deeper understanding of our emotions and the healing process ahead. Here are some questions to contemplate before starting the journey of healing:

- What emotions am I currently experiencing, and how do they impact my daily life?

- Are there past hurts or traumas that still hold power over me, affecting my present well-being?
- How do I typically cope with challenging emotions, and are my coping strategies healthy and effective?
- Do I feel connected to myself and others, or do I struggle to form and maintain meaningful relationships?
- Am I prepared to confront the pain and discomfort that may arise during the healing process?
- What does healing mean to me personally, and what are my intentions for embarking on this journey?
- Can I cultivate self-compassion and patience to navigate the inevitable ups and downs of the healing process?

As we honestly explore these questions, we deepen our self-awareness and readiness for the transformative journey of emotional healing. Embrace these questions as invitations to delve into the depths of your emotions and uncover the resilience and strength that lie within you.

Stages of Emotional Healing

After experiencing deep emotional turmoil, one often finds themselves amidst debris that needs clearing. Memories of the past haunt, stealing peace of mind. Emotional healing demands conscious effort to gather the shattered fragments of oneself into a cohesive whole.

This process unfolds in stages, with each stage requiring patience and skill:

Emotional suffering stems from denying or disregarding painful emotions. In the journey of emotional healing, it's crucial to surrender to this suffering rather than attempting to evade or suppress it. Embrace your pain without judgment. Allow yourself to fully experience the rhythm, vibration, and essence of your emotions. Understanding and feeling your emotions are essential steps toward healing.

Increasing self-awareness of one's emotions involves identifying and acknowledging what one is feeling, why they are feeling it, and how it manifests. This heightened awareness serves as a catalyst for addressing negative emotions constructively. By understanding one's emotional landscape, individuals are inclined towards resolving discomfort in a healthy manner, fostering acceptance and tolerance of their emotional experiences.

This process is particularly crucial in addressing feelings of sadness and anxiety. It entails taking actionable steps to comprehend and navigate the depths of one's emotional turmoil. Armed with insight into their emotions, individuals are better equipped to manage them effectively.

The next stage, named confrontation, entails directly addressing emotional pain rather than avoiding it. This step brings relief, as evading issues typically exacerbates them. Embracing the emotional challenges one has been sidestepping is key to progress. Engaging in honest self-reflection aids in dissecting emotional complexities, identifying triggers, and courageously confronting them. By squarely facing negative emotions, individuals learn to acknowledge and eventually alleviate them, paving the way for emotional healing.

Following the confrontation of painful emotions, there often arises a tendency to avoid them. However, in this stage, it's imperative to honor one's pain by allowing for its expression. Healing necessitates the authentic articulation of emotions, whether it's shedding tears in times of sorrow or venting anger through vocal release.

This cathartic process yields a sense of relief, offering oneself a safe and uninterrupted space to fully experience and express their emotions. Procrastinating this expression risks internalizing emotions, potentially leading to mental fatigue and withdrawal. Through patience and the passage of time, one edges closer to recovery.

The subsequent stage, acceptance, embodies a sense of emotional emptiness. It may feel as though the painful experiences have become ingrained within one's being. However, embracing these undesirable emotions signifies mastery over them, marking a significant step towards emotional healing.

The pain has dissipated, freeing your present thoughts and emotions from its grip. With the struggle behind you, growth begins to unfold. This phase tests your emotional resilience, drawing out your inner strength. As old habits fade, you embrace change with open arms. Through emotional healing, a new life filled with hope and optimism comes within reach.

The Emotional Healing Process involves treating yourself with compassion and kindness during an emotional detox. Acknowledge all your feelings as valid and deserving of attention, bolstering your confidence. Practice self-forgiveness and extend forgiveness to others for circumstances beyond human control.

Nurture your relationships to foster spiritual growth. Release yourself from the burden of past mistakes, focusing instead on cultivating a fulfilling life marked by optimism and personal development. Embrace your true self and engage in activities that bring you joy and fulfillment from within.

Several signs signify that you have successfully navigated through your emotional trauma:

- Acceptance of past difficulties as an integral part of your journey, without denial or avoidance.
- Increased ability to recognize and process your emotions, viewing them as valuable messages for personal growth.
- Diminished fear of previously intimidating situations.
- Heightened sense of happiness and vitality, as if a positive shift is imminent.
- Initiating significant life changes, such as pursuing a new job or renovating your living space.
- Handling disappointments with resilience and adaptability without easily succumbing to upset.
- Understanding that challenging times are transient, with optimism for better days ahead.
- Rediscovery of peace and contentment, leading to improved sleep quality.
- Forgetting to take prescribed medication occasionally, indicating inner strength and wellness.
- Experience of positive and serene thoughts dominating your mind.
- Decreased inclination to dwell on past suffering, focusing instead on personal development.
- Improvement in strained relationships, fostering a desire for healthy connections with loved ones.
- Gradual improvement in physical health, marked by relief from ailments like headaches and sleep disturbances.
- Reduction or absence of physical symptoms such as bodily aches, numbness, or tingling.
- Viewing past experiences as stepping stones toward future growth and opportunity.
- Alleviation of feelings of loneliness and depression, replaced by joy and a positive outlook.
- Rekindled enjoyment of life, signaling progress in the healing journey.

Facilitating emotional healing is a profound journey that demands a compassionate and intentional approach to self-discovery and recovery. It begins with the validation of one's emotions, acknowledging the depth of emotional wounds and allowing space for the experience of sadness. Seeking support from friends, support groups, or holistic practices like prayer coupled meditation proves invaluable in navigating coping strategies.

Granting oneself breaks from distressing experiences and engaging in creative pursuits tailored to personal preferences offer solace and rejuvenation. Embracing adversity as an opportunity for growth and learning, coupled with exercising patience in the gradual healing process, forms the foundation for lasting emotional well-being.

Prioritizing self-care and compassion involves attuning to emotions without judgment, fostering love and care for oneself. Identifying root causes and understanding underlying triggers empower individuals to release pent-up emotions and embark on effective treatment pathways. Cultivating mindfulness, embracing the present moment, and transitioning from victimhood to survivorship further contribute to inner peace and contentment, marking a transformative path towards emotional healing.

Emotional healing plays a pivotal role in promoting holistic well-being, impacting both physical and emotional dimensions and reducing the likelihood of illness. This transformative process contributes to overall health and yields several profound benefits.

Addressing emotional wounds fosters enhanced confidence and self-esteem, laying the foundation for a brighter and more empowered future. The purification of the soul through emotional healing empowers individuals to release trapped wounds, facilitating inner strength and resilience. In turn, contributes to improved interpersonal relationships by fostering empathy and understanding through attunement to one's own emotions.

Emotional healing also acts as a catalyst for forgiveness, leading to personal growth and transformation, shaping individuals into more compassionate and evolved beings. It serves as a means to alleviate emotional pain and tension, providing a profound sense of relief and liberation.

Furthermore, the journey of emotional healing cultivates increased emotional maturity, enabling individuals to navigate relationships with composure and maturity. It promotes deepened self-awareness, unveiling various emotional responses and fostering introspection.

With emotional healing come enhanced decision-making skills rooted in clarity of mind and emotional balance. This transformative process instills a positive outlook towards life, offering a sense of control and emotional equilibrium, ultimately contributing to a more fulfilling and balanced existence. Emotional healing is a dynamic force that transcends individual well-being, radiating positive effects across various facets of life.

Emotional healing stands as a cornerstone in the pursuit of disease prevention and holistic well-being, impacting both the physical and emotional realms and reducing the likelihood of illness while nurturing overall health.

Addressing emotional wounds plays a transformative role in boosting confidence and self-esteem, illuminating a path toward a brighter and more empowered future. It serves as a form of soul cleansing, empowering individuals to release trapped wounds through the purifying strength of tears, fostering inner resilience and strength.

In the context of relationships, being attuned to one's emotions becomes a powerful tool for cultivating healthier and more meaningful connections with others, fostering empathy and understanding emotional healing acts as a catalyst for forgiveness, paving the way for personal growth and transformation, molding individuals into more compassionate and evolved beings.

As part of this healing journey, the alleviation of emotional pain and tension becomes possible, bringing about a profound sense of relief and liberation. The process promotes increased emotional maturity, enabling individuals to navigate relationships with composure, fostering harmonious connections.

Furthermore, emotional healing allows for a deepened self-awareness, unveiling various emotional responses and promoting introspection. It enhances decision-making skills through clarity of mind rooted in self-awareness and emotional balance.

Ultimately, emotional healing cultivates a positive outlook towards life, instilling a sense of control and emotional equilibrium that fosters a more fulfilling and balanced existence. In its comprehensive impact on the individual, emotional healing emerges as a vital force that not only prevents disease but also nurtures holistic well-being.

Opting to address emotional wounds stemming from past hurts and let downs and embracing acceptance and self-awareness marks a significant stride toward personal healing. By releasing emotional barriers and uncertainties, the soul embarks on a journey towards development and overall wellness.

Resilience and Faith

In our discussion of healing, we must underscore the concept of resilience. Resilience is the ability to rebound from adversity and trauma. It's a quality that can be nurtured and fortified through faith and a profound connection with God. In Philippians 4:13, we find inspiration: "I can do all things through Christ who strengthens me." This verse reminds us that, with God's strength, we can overcome even the most daunting emotional challenges.

Hope: The Beacon in the Storm

Amidst the emotional turbulence, hope emerges as a guiding light. Hope is the belief that healing is attainable, that emotional wounds can mend, and that a brighter future awaits. In Romans 15:13, we find encouragement: "May the God of hope fill you with all joy and peace as you trust in him, so that you may overflow with hope by the power of the Holy Spirit." This verse reassures us that God is the source of our hope and that His Spirit empowers us to endure and recover.

In conclusion, the book's exploration of emotional wounds from trauma underscores the profound impact that such wounds can have on our lives. Understanding trauma, including ACEs, provides valuable insights into the sources of these wounds. Through the lens of Scripture, we find comfort in the knowledge that God is close to the brokenhearted and that healing is achievable through faith and resilience. As we traverse the storm of emotional wounds, we are buoyed by the beacon of hope, guiding us toward a future filled with healing and wholeness.(see attachment for ACE questionnaire.

"The Lord is near to the brokenhearted and saves the crushed in spirit." – Psalm 34:18

The Emotional Wounds:

Traumatic experiences often leave emotional wounds that fester beneath the surface. These wounds may manifest as anxiety, depression, anger, or a sense of numbness. One additional manifestation can be foreboding, a feeling of impending doom or apprehension about the future. Foreboding is often labeled as anxiety, but it is distinct in its sense of foretelling something negative.

"The Lord is near to the brokenhearted and saves those who are crushed in spirit." – Psalm 34:18

Understanding Foreboding: Foreboding is characterized by a persistent sense of unease as if a dark cloud looms on the horizon. It is a feeling of impending danger or doom, even when there is no immediate threat. This emotional response can be particularly distressing, as it keeps individuals trapped in a state of constant vigilance, where they are always on the lookout for signs of danger, real or imagined.

 This verse from Proverbs emphasizes the impact of anxious thoughts and forebodings on one's life, contrasting it with the joy and contentment that a glad heart can bring, even in the face of difficulties. It highlights the importance of maintaining a positive and joyful outlook despite challenging circumstances.

All of the verses underscore the heavy burden that anxiety, including foreboding, can place on the human heart. However, it also highlights the power of a kind and comforting word to bring joy and relief. Through faith and the support of others, we can find solace and liberation from the weight of foreboding, allowing us to move toward healing and wholeness.

Scriptural Comfort:

"But I trust in you, O Lord; I say, 'You are my God.'" – Psalm 31:14

"Peace I leave with you; my peace I give to you. Not as the world gives do I give to you. Let not your hearts be troubled, neither let them be afraid." – John 14:27

Biblical Reference to Foreboding: In the book of Proverbs, we find a reference to the concept of foreboding:

"Anxiety in a man's heart weighs him down, but a good word makes him glad." – Proverbs 12:25 (ESV)

"All the days of the desponding and afflicted are made evil [by anxious thoughts and forebodings], but he who has a glad heart has a continual feast [regardless of circumstances]."

Strategies for Processing Traumatic Experiences

To unravel the intricacies of traumatic memories, we require a toolkit of strategies that empower us to navigate these experiences. Psychological experts and research offer valuable insights in this regard. Dr. Bessel van der Kolk, a renowned psychiatrist, underscores the significance of therapies like EMDR (Eye Movement Desensitization and Reprocessing) and somatic experiencing in trauma healing. These therapies harness the body's innate ability to heal and integrate traumatic memories.

As Dr. van der Kolk aptly puts it, "The body keeps the score," emphasizing that if trauma remains unprocessed within us, it can leave an indelible mark, impacting our emotional and physical well-being. Dr. Judith Herman, a trailblazer in trauma studies, emphasizes the importance of creating a safe space for survivors to share their stories. Her book "Trauma and Recovery" highlights the healing power of narrative.

Finding Hope and Restoration through Self-Compassion

In the battle against our adversaries, self-hate is one of the most formidable foes we encounter. It's an unrelenting force that can lead us down a treacherous path, causing us to internalize the lies whispered by oppressing spirits within us. Furthermore, self-hate can exacerbate the trauma we've endured, deepening the emotional wounds we carry.

The Power of Self-Hate: Self-hate operates insidiously and destructively. It turns us into our harshest critics, perpetually replaying past mistakes and perceived flaws in our minds. This self-condemnation nourishes the falsehoods that we are unlovable, unworthy, and irrevocably broken. It's a vicious cycle that ensnares us in a self-constructed prison.

The influence of self-loathing on mental and emotional well-being is profound. When individuals internalize a narrative portraying themselves as "bad" or "wrong," it shapes their thoughts, emotions, and actions.

It's important to acknowledge that perception influences our cognitive and emotional responses, creating a cyclical pattern. Conversely, recognizing our strengths and capabilities tends to enhance self-esteem and confidence.

However, when we fixate on perceived flaws or shortcomings, we're prone to adopting exaggerated negative thoughts, exacerbating our feelings of inadequacy. This negative self-perception can lead to a sense of unworthiness and discomfort in social interactions, hindering the development and maintenance of meaningful relationships.

Self-loathing acts as a pervasive toxin, infiltrating various aspects of life and draining joy and happiness. Seeking support to challenge and reshape these destructive thoughts, focusing on healing, forgiveness, and cultivating hope, is crucial for establishing healthy life foundations and fostering the desired future.

The Lies We Embrace: When an individual experiences self-hate, it signifies a profound internal struggle that can have far-reaching consequences. This emotional state opens the door to the influence of evil spiritual forces, often referred to as "oppressing spirits." These spirits represent the internalized voices and societal pressures that contribute to the deterioration of one's self-worth.

In the grip of self-hate, individuals are vulnerable to accepting falsehoods about themselves. They may begin to adopt distorted perspectives that convince them they deserve the suffering they've endured. This self-blame can manifest as the belief that they are inherently flawed, fundamentally unworthy, or beyond the possibility of healing. The lies perpetuated by these oppressing spirits create a toxic narrative that takes root in the individual's psyche.

As these false beliefs become ingrained, they permeate every aspect of the person's self-perception. The distorted lens through which they view themselves warps their understanding of reality. The individual may struggle to recognize their strengths, accomplishments, and positive attributes, overshadowed by the pervasive conviction that they are inherently damaged.

The distortion caused by self-hate not only affects how individuals perceive themselves but also influences their interactions with the external world. Social relationships, opportunities, and personal growth can be hindered as the individual grapples with a skewed sense of their own value and potential.

Breaking free from this cycle of self-hate involves challenging and dismantling these ingrained falsehoods. It requires a conscious effort to reevaluate self-perceptions, recognize the inherent worth within oneself, and cultivate hope for healing. Seeking support from friends, family, or mental health professionals becomes crucial in navigating this challenging journey toward self-acceptance and emotional well-being.**Exacerbating Trauma:** Self-hate not only perpetuates the trauma we've undergone but also amplifies its effects. It deepens the emotional scars, making it even more challenging to find relief from the pain. Instead of seeking help or reaching out to others, we isolate ourselves, convinced that we are undeserving of support and love.

The Path to Healing: How do we break free from this destructive cycle? The answer lies in self-compassion.

Self-Compassion: Self-compassion entails treating ourselves with the same kindness, understanding, and forgiveness that we would readily extend to a dear friend facing similar challenges. It means recognizing our imperfections without judgment and embracing our inherent humanity.

Biblical Inspiration: The Bible offers profound wisdom regarding the power of compassion, including self-compassion. In Matthew 22:39, Jesus instructs us to "love your neighbor as yourself," implying that self-love and compassion are prerequisites for loving others fully.

A Step toward Healing: Embracing self-compassion isn't a sign of weakness but a courageous stride toward healing. It empowers us to challenge the lies we've internalized, replacing them with the truth of our intrinsic worth and the promise of restoration.

Breaking Free from Self-Hate: It's time to shatter the chains of self-hate and liberate ourselves from the clutches of our inner oppressing spirits. By practicing self-compassion, we can discover hope and restoration, no matter how profound our wounds are. This journey demands patience and perseverance, but it's a path well worth taking.

You Are Worthy of Love and Healing: Always remember you are deserving of love, healing, and restoration. Your past does not dictate your future, and your scars can become a testament to your strength and resilience. Let self-compassion illuminate your journey to reclaiming your life and finding hope amidst the darkness.

Understanding Self-Compassion: Self-compassion allows us to realize that we are not defined by our traumatic experiences. It involves forgiving ourselves for any perceived shortcomings and embracing the truth that we did the best we could with the resources available to us at the time.

Hope and Restoration: Through self-compassion, we uncover hope and restoration. We acknowledge that healing is attainable and that God's grace is sufficient to mend even the deepest wounds. Just as Joseph forgave his brothers for their betrayal and found reconciliation, we can experience healing and reconciliation within ourselves too.

"And now do not be distressed or angry with yourselves because you sold me here, for God sent me before you to preserve life." – Genesis 45:5

In this profound journey through the shadows of trauma, we navigate the emotional wounds left behind and employ strategies that empower us to process these experiences. Through self-compassion, we find the hope and restoration needed to reclaim our lives. Remember that, like the phoenix that rises from its own ashes, you can emerge from the darkness of trauma into the light of healing and wholeness too.

"For I know the plans I have for you, declares the Lord, plans for welfare and not for evil, to give you a future and a hope." – Jeremiah 29:11

Until we cultivate self-compassion, we fail to truly love ourselves. This lack of self-love lies at the root of our spiritual, emotional, mental, and physical wounds. When we are disconnected from self-love, we sense a disconnection from our source, which is love itself. Initiating a dialogue with our source, acknowledging our wounds, and embracing responsibility for our lives are crucial steps towards healing and well-being.

Often, intense negative emotions signal the activation of old childhood wounds. At such times, a gateway to our unconscious beckons us to confront and heal these wounds. Our conditioned response may urge us to avoid this gateway, seeking solace in addictive substances or behaviors. Yet, when the pain becomes unbearable, we may seek guidance from sources like this one or immerse ourselves in books driven by a deep desire to heal and attain well-being.

All our wounds stem from a false belief in our separation from our source. Ultimately, it is our source that facilitates all healing. Hence, aligning ourselves with it is the primary step in any effective healing endeavor. However, we must also collaborate with the divine, actively participating in our own healing journey.

This entails nurturing self-compassion, which dismantles the core wound that otherwise persists within our spirit beings. For enduring healing, we must acknowledge our wounds consciously and extend love to these vulnerable parts of ourselves, commencing with self-compassion.

Self-compassion entails embracing yourself with deep awareness and without judgment, much like a loyal and reliable friend. It involves being present with yourself as a compassionate companion to your own pain.

This compassionate stance encompasses care, concern, sensitivity, warmth, unconditional love, tenderness, acceptance, mercy, leniency, kindness, and charity towards oneself. Self-compassion infuses a gentle, accepting essence into your emotional wounds, enveloping them with unconditional love and intimate understanding.

No one understands your feelings and hurts as intimately as you do. You possess firsthand knowledge of all the intricacies and nuances of your pain. Therefore, you are uniquely qualified to extend love to these parts of yourself.

Self-compassion involves viewing your most tender wounds without judgment. It means being willing to acknowledge and feel the reality of your pain without attempting to conceal it or immediately "fix" it.

When self-love reaches this depth, it illuminates the reasons behind the pain. Through loving self-compassion, awareness unveils the cause-and-effect dynamics that led to the creation of the wound—a series of circumstances from which negative beliefs about ourselves emerged.

Compassion empowers us to see ourselves as our source sees us. It is a divine quality, granting access to the highest realm of healing and well-being. Through compassion, we intimately experience the unconditional love of our source, feeling completely loved in every aspect of our being. Until we consciously address our own psychological healing and well-being, lingering energetic wounds stemming from a sense of separation from Love persist within our spirit beings.

While the love and compassion of others can aid in our growth by teaching us to open and receive, transformative healing comes from within. At the heart of every wound lies a belief in our separation from God, from Love—a fear of being unworthy of love. This belief is one we have internalized about ourselves.

Only you possess the power to release this belief by experiencing the undeniable truth of your inherent lovability. This is the profound gift of self-compassion. Though external affirmations of our worthiness may uplift us momentarily, the wounded aspect of our psyche clings to beliefs of inadequacy until we affirm our worthiness from within.

No amount of external validation will suffice until we dismantle the core belief of separateness from Love and embrace the truth of our infinite worthiness. This pivotal psychological shift is crucial for lasting healing, preventing the continual re-creation of energetic wounds within us.

Until we confront the root cause of the wound—the belief in separation from our spirit being, from Love—with the truth of our inherent connection and worthiness, it will persist within our souls attracting similar painful experiences into our lives.

Prioritizing ourselves and our healing journey enables us to comprehend the reasons behind our past actions or words that we may not be proud of. We realize that our reactions stem not from inherent "badness" but from pain and a sense of limited options. This realization paves the way for self-compassion and well-being.

For many, the concept of self-compassion is unfamiliar territory, rarely modeled or taught during childhood or even in adulthood. Every instance of emotional pain in our present lives presents an opportunity to cultivate self-compassion and engage in deep, intimate self-reflection. By delving into this introspection, we unearth the core shame that resides within each of us, offering us the chance to heal it.

Self-compassion is akin to nourishment for the starving soul. As you begin to experience your own love, you come to realize the immense burden in seeking love and compassion from external sources. No matter how much external validation you receive, it never seems to be sufficient.

This inadequacy persists because external affirmations cannot alter your inner beliefs. If someone else professes your wonderfulness while deep down, perhaps unconsciously, you deny it, their love merely acts as a temporary salve. Soon enough, you'll find yourself seeking more validation from them or others, perpetuating the cycle of seeking external validation.

True fulfillment comes from self-compassion and self-love, filling the inner void created by the false belief of being unlovable. Extending compassion to yourself allows you to directly experience, for yourself and about yourself, your inherent lovability and the love that surrounds you.

This firsthand experience dismantles old false beliefs on spiritual, emotional, and psychological levels. Consequently, your level of spiritual contemptment shifts, leading to tangible changes in your physical well-being, as the physical, emotional and mental diseases re released from your body soul and spirit beings.

After a lifetime of habitually judging ourselves, it's natural for self-judgment to arise if we don't immediately grasp this process or can't complete it all at once (which is the case for most people). The key is to simply begin from where you are.

In instances of severe trauma, discussions about self-compassion might seem foreign or overwhelming. In such cases, it's perfectly acceptable to start with just one aspect that resonates with you and take it step by step. Each step will naturally lead you to the next and then the next.

As you implement these suggestions for cultivating self-compassion, be prepared for it to take time. This type of Healing typically occurs gradually, one step at a time. Some deeply ingrained memories may require more time and patience to sit with and accept the associated feelings, so don't judge yourself for the pace of your progress. Offer compassion wherever you are in the process and work from that point.

Being kind and gentle with yourself, regardless of your inner turmoil, is an act of self-compassion. All the coping mechanisms we've adopted—such as withdrawing, projecting our feelings onto others, or acting out—are strategies devised by a part of our psyche attempting to shield the inner vulnerable child within us in the only way it knows how.

By embracing self-compassion, a profound psychological healing takes place. Our psyche no longer feels the need to resort to defensive measures once it recognizes that we're finally tending to the needs of the inner child in a nurturing manner.

As you continue practicing self-compassion, you'll notice an expansion of inner space and a greater sense of well-being. You'll feel more liberated to express yourself authentically. By nurturing your inner child and fostering self-love, you'll experience genuine self-empowerment and develop a stronger sense of self-trust.

Consequently, you'll establish healthier boundaries with others and rely less on them for your well-being. As your self-love grows, you notice and cultivate more joyful and uplifting experiences into your life.

Another beautiful outcome of practicing self-compassion is that compassion for others will flow naturally and effortlessly. Once you've intimately experienced compassion for yourself, you'll have an abundance of it to share with others.

Chapter 6:　　Embracing Healing: Overcoming the Weight of Self-Rejection

Insights from Christian Authors on Emotional Healing

In your pursuit of emotional healing, delving into the wisdom of Christian authors can provide profound enlightenment and invaluable support. These writers skillfully blend the Gospel's truths with practical insights to help navigate life's emotional challenges. Personally, I have found their works to be immensely helpful as I embarked on my own journey to untangle the knots that hindered my progress on the path to healing.

One such transformative book that has left a lasting impact is "Emotionally Healthy Spirituality" by Peter Scazzero. Within the pages of this profound work, Scazzero explores the vital connection between emotional health and spiritual maturity. He underscores the notion that authentic spiritual growth necessitates a deep dive into our emotional well-being, compelling us to confront unresolved issues from our past. By embracing this journey, we unlock the potential for a richer, more authentic relationship with God, leading to genuine transformation.

Scazzero's book serves as a guiding light for readers, encouraging them to recognize the profound influence of emotional wounds on their spiritual lives. He provides practical, actionable guidance on breaking free from destructive patterns, nurturing healthier relationships, and fostering emotional maturity that aligns with one's faith. By weaving emotional health into the fabric of spirituality, Scazzero presents a pathway to a more vibrant and fulfilling Christian life.

In addition to the authors previously mentioned—Frank Hammond, Joyce Meyer, and Neil T. Anderson—Pastor Tony Kemp's books also offer valuable insights into emotional healing and spiritual growth. Kemp's works, such as "Unlocked: Keys to Experiencing God's Presence" and "The Supernatural You," delve into the profound connection between spirituality and emotional well-being. His teachings emphasize the importance of recognizing and addressing emotional barriers to achieve a deeper relationship with God.

These Christian authors collectively contribute to the wealth of wisdom available to those seeking emotional and spiritual healing. They empower readers to find solace, discover direction, and experience enduring healing on their unique journeys. I believe many individuals are searching for insight and wisdom to identify and articulate the knots hindering their progress. Therefore, I highly recommend exploring the books recommended by these authors to gain valuable guidance and support.

Navigating the Journey of Self-Acceptance

The journey towards self-acceptance is a sacred path, pivotal to realizing the fullness of our identity as crafted by God, the Creator. In the image of God, each of us is intricately designed, reflecting His glory and complexity. Yet, life's entanglements—those knots within our minds and hearts—can obscure the clear view of our true selves, the image in which we were lovingly made.

Self-acceptance means seeing oneself through the lens of grace and love with which God views us. It is an acknowledgment of our inherent worth that comes from being His creation. Scripture reminds us in Genesis 1:27 that we are made in God's image. This divine blueprint bestows upon us a value beyond comparison, a blueprint that holds the potential for greatness inherent in our design.

However, the knots of self-doubt, criticism, and rejection can distort this vision. They are the lies that whisper we are not enough, the shadows that suggest we fall short. But the truth remains steadfast; we are fearfully and wonderfully made, as Psalm 139:14 confirms. Untangling these knots is not merely an act of personal development but a spiritual imperative. It is a process of peeling back the layers of falsehood and coming face-to-face with the masterpiece that is our true self.

In this untangling, we find that self-acceptance is more than just an exercise in positivity. It is a form of worship, recognition of the God's work within us. It is about embracing every aspect of our being, even imperfections, as part of a grander design. When we accept ourselves, we align with God's view of us, acknowledging that we are "his workmanship, created in Christ Jesus for good works" (Ephesians 2:10).

Embracing self-acceptance allows us to live more fully in the freedom for which Christ has set us free (Galatians 5:1). It liberates us from the bondage of self-rejection and empowers us to step into the identity God has ordained for us. As we learn to see ourselves as God sees us, we are enabled to cast off the chains that hold us back and step into the light of truth.

Thus, the importance of self-acceptance cannot be overstated. It is the key that unlocks the door to our true potential, the mirror that reflects our divine heritage. As we walk the path of untangling our knots, let us do so with the assurance that on the other side lies a clearer vision of our true selves—beloved, accepted, and wholly embraced by the One who created us.

Within each individual exists a shadow—a compilation of concealed facets, wounds, and vulnerabilities often suppressed or disavowed. Yet, when we embrace our shadows through self-acceptance, it can lead to profound healing and personal metamorphosis. Let's delve into the potency of self-acceptance in embracing our shadows, acknowledging our past, and attaining inner completeness.

Our shadows symbolize the parts of ourselves that we perceive as undesirable or unacceptable. They may originate from past traumas, unresolved wounds, or facets of our character that we've pushed aside. By acknowledging and delving into our shadows, we embark on a journey to comprehend their influence on our lives and unlock the potential for healing.

Embracing our shadows demands great courage and vulnerability. It entails confronting the aspects of ourselves that we've evaded or disowned. Through self-acceptance, we cultivate the fortitude to confront our reality, embracing our shadows as indispensable components of our journey and catalysts for personal growth.

Self-acceptance lays the groundwork for self-compassion, providing a nurturing environment for healing. As we embrace our shadows with gentleness and empathy, we relinquish the weight of self-condemnation and shame. Self-compassion enables us to integrate our shadows, fostering internal healing and fostering a sense of wholeness.

Embracing our shadows initiates a process of integration and self-exploration. As we recognize and embrace all facets of ourselves, we unveil hidden strengths, resilience, and wisdom within our shadows. This journey leads to a deeper self-understanding and a heightened sense of authenticity.

Self-acceptance transcends our individual journey; it also shapes our relationships. By embracing our shadows, we cultivate a space for vulnerability and genuineness in our interactions with others. We allow ourselves to be seen and accepted, nurturing deeper and more meaningful connections founded on trust and empathy.

Embracing our shadows through self-acceptance is a profound act of healing and self-discovery. We embark on a path toward wholeness and authenticity by acknowledging and incorporating our concealed aspects, wounds, and vulnerabilities.

Through self-compassion, bravery, and the courage to confront our truth, we unleash the transformative potential of self-acceptance. Let us embrace our shadows, for within them lies the gateway to profound healing, personal evolution, and a life lived authentically.

Self-acceptance is a journey, not a destination. If you find yourself in the category of "almost healed, but not quite," know that you are not alone. Many survivors of child abuse or trauma experience this frustrating limbo, unsure of why they can't seem to fully move forward.

Most survivors I have worked with, and those that I've encountered, endured prolonged abuse. The longer we suffer in silence, burying our stories, the harder it becomes to initiate change. The beginning stages of change are always the most challenging. You've grown accustomed to living with your past, knowing how to navigate it, but facing something new is daunting because it's unfamiliar. However, if you're feeling exhausted and yearning for change, you're likely ready to take the necessary steps.

Escaping the "almost but not quite healed" phase is possible, but it requires time, commitment, and courage, starting with acceptance. When I mention acceptance, I'm not suggesting you should justify the abuse you endured—it was never acceptable. Instead, I urge you to accept yourself and the truth of your experience.

The truth is, someone you knew and trusted hurt you. To survive that abuse, you likely internalized the belief that it was somehow your fault. Without anyone to counter this belief, it became deeply ingrained, convincing you that you were undeserving of love and care.

Living a fulfilling life feels impossible when you carry such heavy feelings of unworthiness. I understand this struggle intimately. I battled with myself constantly, desiring things I thought I couldn't have while feeling fundamentally unworthy due to the abuse I suffered and the actions I took to cope. It seemed inconceivable that I could ever view myself with kindness, let alone love and respect myself.

But I did achieve it, and I want to share with you, my friend, that you can too. Once I grasped the internal conflict within myself and understood why I believed I was unworthy (because I hadn't experienced anything different), I began to feel a shift. I embarked on the difficult task of delving deep and examining every reason my wounded self believed I couldn't heal or be restored, why I felt I was unlovable. Each time, another reason arose.

I sat with myself and my inner child or younger self. I sat with him and listened attentively. I acknowledged his feelings and the reasons behind them. I assured him that despite his beliefs or perceived flaws, I accepted him. Not only did I accept him, but I loved him. I allowed the Lord to envelope him in loving warmth.

By accepting the darkest parts of myself, I discovered the best within me. I became the nurturing, loving person that I desperately needed. I fought for the best version of myself.

I learned about my courage and strength, my capacity for deep feelings, and my compassion for myself and others. It's challenging at times, but through this process, I learned not to fear my emotions. They hold wisdom and foster connection—the connection I yearned for, which I found within myself and finally made sense.

This journey of understanding and accepting all parts of myself tested me, as it test the people that I work with. But gradually, with time, I truly began to feel the love. I started to feel love for myself and trust in that love. It remains a process I continue to use daily. You can utilize it to heal yourself, my friend. I believe in you. We can all heal from the terrible things that happened to us. And together, we can accomplish it.

In a society we are inundated with notions of perfection and conformity, embracing oneself becomes an act of bravery. It entails loving and embracing who you are, flaws and all, without seeking validation from others.

When we release self-rejection, we unlock a realm of liberation and joy. Embracing oneself holds significance because it fosters self-esteem, confronts the inner critic, cultivates self-compassion, and establishes a support system.

It's about honoring your unique attributes, embracing imperfections, and shedding the stifling veil of perfectionism. Trust me, embarking on this journey is a breath of fresh air you won't regret.

Biblical Inspirations for Overcoming Rejection

"Rejection is a wound that needs healing. In the loving arms of our Savior, we find acceptance and belonging," Hammond reminds us. Dealing with self-rejection is often one of the most significant knots we must unravel on our journey to wholeness. It's a painful and burdensome weight that can hinder our progress and keep us from realizing our true potential. But, as Hammond's wisdom reminds us, healing is possible through the loving embrace of our Savior.

The Weight of Self-Rejection: Self-rejection is a heavy burden to carry. It whispers in our ears that we are not good enough, don't belong, and are fundamentally flawed. These lies can be paralyzing, trapping us in a cycle of self-doubt and insecurity.

The Healing Power of Faith: As we delve into Hammond's teachings and other resources on emotional healing, we discover that faith plays a vital role in our journey. The Bible tells us in Psalm 34:18 that "The Lord is near to the brokenhearted and saves those who are crushed in spirit." This verse reminds us that God is with us in our pain and is ready to bring healing to our wounded hearts.

Practical Steps to Healing: Hammond's book offers practical steps to heal from the pain of rejection. It aligns with the principles of faith and self-compassion, guiding us toward a path of self-acceptance and belonging. By embracing these principles, we can begin to untangle the knots of self-rejection and find the freedom to be our true selves.

Unraveling the Rejection

Isaiah 53:3 (NIV): "He was despised and rejected by mankind, a man of suffering, and familiar with pain. Like one from whom people hide their faces he was despised, and we held him in low esteem." This verse reminds us that even Jesus, our Savior, experienced rejection. He understands our pain and is there to heal our wounds.

1 Peter 2:4 (NIV): "As you come to him, the living Stone—rejected by humans but chosen by God and precious to him." We are chosen and precious to God, regardless of any rejection we may have faced.

You Are Not Alone: On this journey of healing, remember that you are not alone. The support of knowledgeable authors like Frank Hammond and the comforting presence of our Savior is with you every step of the way. As you delve into these resources and Scripture, you will find the tools you need to break free from the chains of self-rejection and embrace the love and acceptance that have always been available to you.

Scripture Comfort:

"The Lord is near to the brokenhearted and saves the crushed in spirit." – Psalm 34:18

"I sought the Lord, and he answered me and delivered me from all my fears." – Psalm 34:4

"Cast your burden on the Lord, and he will sustain you; he will never permit the righteous to be moved." – Psalm 55:22

"Peace I leave with you; my peace I give to you. Not as the world gives do I give to you. Let not your hearts be troubled, neither let them be afraid." – John 14:27

"But I trust in you, O Lord; I say, 'You are my God.'" – Psalm 31:14

Amid the shadows of trauma, self-compassion is the beacon of light that guides us toward hope and restoration. Self-compassion involves extending the same kindness and understanding to ourselves that we offer to others.

"But he said to me, 'My grace is sufficient for you, for my power is made perfect in weakness.'" – 2 Corinthians 12:9

For the remainder of the book, I am praying for the Holy Spirit to guide us as we continue tackling the knots. Let's pray:

Heavenly Father, first we give you thanks for all that you continue to do. We know that you are perfect and your desire if for us to be able to be one with you. We confess that we have had things that happened to us that we have not been able to resolve that it has fully worked for our good. We ask you know that you will help us to resolve the knots that prevent us from readily accessing your goodness in our memories. We ask this in the name of Jesus and we receive by faith.

Self-rejection is akin to hosting a pity party where enjoyment is conspicuously absent.B I've had firsthand experience with it.

Ever caught you thinking why did I just embarrass myself in front of everyone? Oh right, because I'm a disaster. That's self-rejection in all its cringe-worthy glory. It's that relentless cycle of doubting your abilities, diminishing yourself, and feeling unworthy.

Why do we fall prey to self-rejection? Past encounters with harsh criticism or brutal rejection can leave scars, making us feel more like a potato than a person. Someone's words once made you doubt your value. But really, who needs self-confidence anyway?

Now, brace yourself for the aftermath of this unwelcome visitor: low self-esteem, social anxiety, and sometimes even the specter of depression. You become your own worst critic, berating every mistake and flaw. It's like having an incessant bully in your head that never gives you a break.

Self-rejection is a party you'd rather skip. Let's delve into the journey of freeing ourselves from its grip.

Breaking free from self-rejection begins with recognizing your inherent worth. Stop diminishing your accomplishments or dismissing compliments as insignificant, especially for mothers juggling business responsibilities, acknowledge your incredible achievements and allow yourself to revel in your successes.

When someone acknowledges your efforts, accept their praise with pride—because you truly deserve it! We all contend with an inner dialogue that feeds us negative beliefs accumulated over time. It's time to bid farewell to that nonsense! Challenge those negative thoughts with tangible evidence.

When you recognize baseless negativity creeping in, flip the script. Remind yourself of your strengths, past achievements, and instances where you defied self-doubt. Witness your inner critic's voice gradually losing its power!

Practicing self-compassion is undeniably transformative. Treat yourself with the same kindness and understanding you would offer a dear friend facing challenges. Embrace your imperfections and recognize that you're a masterpiece in progress. None of us are flawless, and that's the essence of being human.

Lastly, a robust support system can work wonders. Surround yourself with individuals who uplift you and recognize your brilliance even when you struggle to see it yourself. Lean on friends, family, or engage with a community that offers support, reminding you that you're never alone.

None of us are flawless, and that's perfectly okay. In fact, our imperfections add richness and depth to our lives. Consider those unique qualities that define you—your infectious smile or resilience in confronting challenges head-on. Finding beauty in our imperfections is a liberating experience.

It's akin to discovering hidden treasures; it's about cherishing those quirks that paint the canvas of our existence. Instead of striving for an unattainable standard, let's prioritize self-acceptance. Let's celebrate every achievement, no matter how small, and grant ourselves the compassion to embrace our humanity.

Speaking from personal experience as someone who has journeyed from being a perfectionist, let me tell you, perfectionism offers little but promises much. The pursuit of flawlessness can be exhausting, stealing away the genuine joys of life. Let's opt for a different route, where we honor our beautiful imperfections and embrace authenticity in every aspect of life.

And remember, the decision to grow and evolve is personal, driven by your own aspirations, not external pressures. Life is far too precious to waste chasing illusions. Rise up, embrace your uniqueness, and let your wonderful imperfections illuminate the world.

Celebrating your authentic self is acknowledging that these quirks are intricately woven into the fabric of your being, adding a touch of brilliance to your personality. And you know what? That's exactly what makes you, you—a rare blend of uniqueness and charm.

Chapter 7:   Giving and Receiving Help in the Healing Process

Spiritual life coaching is a transformative practice aimed at facilitating individuals in connecting with their inner selves, enhancing their spiritual awareness, and seeking guidance on their life's path. It blends conventional coaching methodologies with spiritual principles to empower individuals to access their inner wisdom and harmonize their actions with their higher calling. In this segment, we'll delve into the essence of spiritual life coaching and its advantages.

What Does Spiritual Life Coaching Entail? Spiritual life coaching is a specialized coaching approach centered around the spiritual dimensions of an individual's existence. It acknowledges that spirituality is a profoundly personal and diverse journey, endeavoring to aid individuals in exploring, comprehending, and nurturing their spiritual essence.

A spiritual life coach assumes the role of a mentor, offering a nurturing and non-judgmental environment for individuals to delve into their spiritual convictions, values, and purpose. They assist clients in identifying and surmounting any barriers impeding their spiritual growth and guide them in crafting a life that resonates with their spiritual beliefs.

In contrast to therapy or counseling, which often focuses on resolving past traumas, spiritual life coaching is oriented towards the future. It encourages individuals to envision their desired future, establish meaningful objectives, and take inspired steps towards materializing their aspirations. Spiritual life coaching is especially beneficial for those seeking to deepen their spiritual bond with God, augment their self-awareness, and discover greater purpose and satisfaction in life.

The importance of giving and receiving help in the healing process, especially for inner wounds and spiritual healing, is significant. Both giving and receiving help play crucial roles in fostering emotional, psychological, and spiritual well-being. Here's a breakdown of their importance:

Giving Help:

Empowerment: Offering assistance to others can empower you and the person receiving help. It reinforces a sense of purpose and contribution, which is essential for spiritual growth.

Connection: Helping others creates meaningful connections and strengthens social bonds. This sense of connection is vital for spiritual healing, as it provides a support system and a sense of belonging.

Gratitude: The act of giving help often leads to feelings of gratitude. Cultivating gratitude is a powerful spiritual practice that can enhance overall well-being and contribute to inner healing.

Generosity: Generosity is a spiritual virtue that transcends self-centeredness. Giving help allows you to embody this virtue, promoting a more expansive and compassionate state of being.

Receiving Help:

Vulnerability: Allowing oneself to receive help requires vulnerability, an essential aspect of spiritual growth. It teaches humility and opens the door to deeper self-awareness and healing.

Mutual Exchange: The act of receiving help creates a reciprocal relationship, fostering a sense of mutual support and interconnectedness.

Self-Compassion: Accepting help is an act of self-compassion. It acknowledges that everyone deserves support and that it is okay to seek assistance in times of need, promoting a healthier relationship with oneself.

Community and Unity: Receiving help builds a sense of community and unity. In the spiritual journey, a supportive community is often seen as a source of strength and inspiration.

In the context of spiritual healing, both giving and receiving help create and completes the biblical principal of sowing and reaping loop, fostering growth, compassion, and a deeper connection with oneself and others. It's a symbiotic relationship that contributes to the holistic well-being of individuals on their spiritual journeys.

The Advantages of Spiritual Life Coaching

- Participating in spiritual life coaching offers a plethora of benefits for individuals striving for personal and spiritual development. Here are some key advantages:
- Clarity and Purpose: Spiritual life coaching assists individuals in gaining clarity regarding their values, interests, and life objectives. Through guided introspection and exploration, clients can deepen their self-awareness and unearth what truly resonates with them.
- Self-Awareness and Mindfulness: Spiritual life coaching fosters self-awareness, enabling individuals to become more mindful of their thoughts, emotions, and actions. This heightened awareness empowers them to make conscious decisions and approach life's hurdles with mindfulness.
- Inner Healing and Transformation: Spiritual life coaching aids individuals in addressing emotional wounds, shedding limiting beliefs, and transcending negative patterns. By delving into the root causes of emotional distress or trauma, individuals can undergo significant healing and personal evolution.
- Alignment and Authenticity: Through spiritual life coaching, individuals are encouraged to embrace their authentic selves, synchronize their actions with their fundamental values, and lead lives true to themselves. This alignment fosters a profound sense of fulfillment and inner tranquility.
- Support and Accountability: A spiritual life coach provides ongoing support, motivation, and accountability throughout the individual's journey. This supportive framework assists clients in maintaining commitment to their objectives, surmounting obstacles, and navigating challenges with resilience.

By partaking in spiritual life coaching, individuals can unlock their innate potential, undergo personal metamorphosis, and lead lives imbued with significance and purpose.

Understanding the Role of a Spiritual Life Coach

Spiritual life coaching is a potent method designed to aid individuals in delving into and enriching their spiritual well-being. Understanding the function of a spiritual life coach and the methodologies they employ is crucial in comprehending the mechanics of this coaching practice.

A spiritual life coach assumes the position of a mentor and coach in an individual's spiritual voyage. They extend support, motivation, and direction to assist clients in connecting with their inner selves, uncovering their life purpose, and nurturing a deeper sense of contentment.

A spiritual life coach establishes a secure and non-judgmental environment for clients to explore their spiritual convictions, values, and encounters. Through active listening, thought-provoking inquiries, and facilitating introspection, they aid clients in attaining clarity and enlightenment.

The role of a spiritual life coach transcends the confines of coaching sessions. They provide continual support and hold clients accountable, empowering them to incorporate spiritual practices and principles into their everyday routines. With their adeptness in spirituality and personal development, spiritual life coaches ignite inspiration and encouragement within clients to embrace their spiritual capabilities.

Approaches and Methods Utilized in Spiritual Life Coaching

Spiritual life coaching encompasses a variety of techniques and methodologies tailored to aid clients on their spiritual odyssey. These techniques, personalized to each individual's distinct requirements, may encompass:

Mindfulness and Prayer coupled with Meditation: Encouraging clients to nurture present-moment awareness and engage in meditation practices to calm the mind, alleviate stress, and augment spiritual connection.

Visualization and Affirmations: Guiding clients in visualizing their desired outcomes and employing positive affirmations to reshape limiting beliefs, fostering a constructive mindset.

Journaling: Advocating for clients to partake in reflective writing exercises to delve into their thoughts, emotions, and spiritual encounters. Journaling serves to deepen self-awareness and enrich the comprehension of one's spiritual journey.

Exploration of Spiritual Teachings and Traditions: Sharing insights from diverse spiritual traditions and teachings to broaden clients' perspectives and deepen their spiritual comprehension.

By deploying these techniques and approaches, spiritual life coaches facilitate clients in unraveling their inner authenticity, harmonizing their actions with biblical and spiritual principles, and experiencing personal evolution and enhancement.

Grasping the workings of spiritual life coaching can provide invaluable guidance and support to individuals embarking on their spiritual voyage. Collaborating with a proficient spiritual life coach empowers individuals to explore their spirituality, attain clarity, and foster a profound inner tranquility and contentment.

When individuals engage in spiritual life coaching, they can anticipate receiving guidance and assistance in various facets of their lives. Here are three fundamental areas commonly addressed in spiritual life coaching:

Discovering Purpose and Meaning: A primary objective of spiritual life coaching involves aiding individuals in uncovering their purpose and deriving meaning from their lives. Through deep introspection and exploration, a spiritual life coach helps clients identify their core values, passions, and unique talents. By aligning their actions with their authentic purpose, individuals can experience heightened fulfillment and satisfaction across all spheres of their lives.

During coaching sessions, clients are prompted to delve into their aspirations, desires, and dreams, facilitating clarity regarding their life's purpose. Utilizing introspective techniques, goal-setting strategies, and guidance from the spiritual life coach, individuals can embark on a journey that resonates with their genuine selves.

Inner Healing and Transformation: Spiritual life coaching delves into the realm of inner healing and personal transformation. Many individuals carry emotional scars, limiting beliefs, and past traumas that impede their personal development and well-being. A spiritual life coach provides clients with a nurturing and supportive environment to explore and heal these deep-seated emotional wounds.

Through diverse therapeutic methods such as mindfulness exercises, visualization, and biblical healing practices, individuals can release emotional barriers and progress towards a state of healing and completeness. As a facilitator, the spiritual life coach assists clients in navigating their internal landscape, uncovering concealed patterns, and facilitating the transformative process.

Fostering Self-Awareness and Mindfulness: Nurturing self-awareness and practicing mindfulness are pivotal aspects of spiritual life coaching. Through the cultivation of self-awareness, individuals attain a deeper comprehension of their thoughts, emotions, and actions. This heightened self-awareness empowers them to make deliberate choices and align their behaviors with their values and intentions.

Mindfulness techniques like prayer coupled with meditation and breathwork aid individuals in connecting with the present moment, fostering inner tranquility and clarity. These practices also enhance stress management, concentration, and overall well-being.

Spiritual life coaching encourages individuals to integrate mindfulness into their daily routines, creating opportunities for self-reflection and self-care. A spiritual life coach may introduce a variety of mindfulness practices and guide clients in incorporating these techniques into their lifestyles.

Exploration of these areas in spiritual life coaching can catalyze profound personal development, heightened self-awareness, and an enhanced sense of purpose and contentment. By collaborating with a spiritual life coach, individuals embark on a transformative journey, aligning external actions with innermost aspirations and desires.

The Qualities of a Spiritual Helper

Helping others untangle the complex knots in their lives is a journey that requires discernment, patience, kindness, and personal experience of transformation. Before embarking on this journey with another, it is vital to prayerfully consider whether one is the right person to offer such help. The path to aiding others in this deeply spiritual and emotional process begins with a self-reflective assessment of our readiness and suitability.

The first step is to seek divine guidance through prayer. This spiritual communication should be aimed at understanding God's will and discerning whether one has been called to serve in this capacity. James 1:5 encourages us to ask God for wisdom generously given to all without finding fault. The clarity that comes from such prayerful consideration will ensure that the help offered is not just well-intentioned but also ordained and blessed for effectiveness.

The person aiming to help must embody certain characteristics epitomized by Christ Himself: patience and kindness. These fruits of the Spirit, as outlined in Galatians 5:22-23, are non-negotiable for someone who intends to assist others in unraveling their internal struggles. Patience allows the helper to give the person unraveling their knots the time they need to process and heal. Kindness ensures that the journey is compassionate, which can make all the difference in someone's healing process.

Moreover, the helper must have navigated their own journey of untangling knots. This isn't to say they must be perfect or have resolved every issue in their life. Still, they should have experienced significant personal victory and freedom in Christ. 2 Corinthians 1:4 speaks of God comforting us in all our troubles so that we can comfort those in any trouble with the comfort we ourselves receive from God. One who has walked through the fire and come out refined is well-positioned to guide others through their flames.

Selecting the ideal spiritual life coach is a significant decision, one that necessitates careful consideration and inquiry. Here are pertinent questions to pose when evaluating potential spiritual life coaches:

- What is your coaching approach? Understanding the coaching methodology of a spiritual life coach provides insight into their techniques and practices. Inquire about their coaching philosophy, tools, and strategies utilized to support clients.
- What is your experience in spiritual coaching? Explore the background and experience of the spiritual life coach in the realm of spiritual coaching. Inquire about their certifications, training, and relevant qualifications that showcase their expertise in the field.
- How do you customize your coaching to individual needs? It's crucial to ascertain whether the spiritual life coach can tailor their approach to meet your specific objectives and requirements. Inquire about how they adapt their coaching style to address the unique facets of each client's spiritual journey.
- What is your availability and coaching structure? Gain insight into the availability and structure of the spiritual life coach's coaching sessions. Inquire about the frequency, duration, and format of sessions and any additional support provided outside of scheduled sessions.
- Can you offer client testimonials or references? Request testimonials or references from previous clients to gain firsthand insights into their experiences working with the spiritual life coach. This can aid in assessing the coach's effectiveness and compatibility with your needs.

Selecting the right spiritual life coach is a personal journey, one that requires thorough research and exploration. Take the time to assess potential coaches, ensuring alignment with your values, goals, and spiritual beliefs. Remember, a compatible coach can provide invaluable guidance and support on your spiritual voyage towards inner peace and growth.

Integrating the Transformative Power of Spiritual Life Coaching

Upon experiencing the transformative influence of spiritual life coaching, it becomes imperative to weave the acquired insights and wisdom into the fabric of your daily existence. This segment will delve into three pivotal aspects of assimilating spiritual life coaching into your life: application of insights, fostering sustained inner peace and growth, and additional resources for spiritual enrichment.

Applying Learning and Insights: To optimize your spiritual life coaching journey, it's paramount to actively employ the learnings and revelations garnered during your sessions. This entails integrating the principles, techniques, and counsel your spiritual life coach provides your everyday life. By doing so, you initiate positive shifts and transformations across various facets of your existence.

Methods to apply learning and insights include:

Embracing mindfulness and self-awareness practices to foster presence and inner connection. Harnessing visualization and affirmation techniques to manifest your aspirations and objectives. Incorporating spiritual rituals or observances that resonate with your convictions and values. Incorporating newfound perspectives and beliefs into your decision-making framework, utilizing spiritual principles to enrich your relationships and interactions with others

Remember, the integration of learning is an ongoing journey necessitating consistency, dedication, and patience as you navigate your individual spiritual odyssey.

Sustaining Inner Peace and Growth A primary aim of spiritual life coaching is to aid individuals in cultivating inner tranquility and nurturing personal development. To sustain these constructive changes, it's imperative to perpetuate the nurturing of your spiritual well-being beyond the coaching sessions.

Consider the Following Tips to Sustain Inner Peace and Growth:

Prioritize self-care and introspection to maintain a profound connection with your inner self. Engage in regular prayer session and mindfulness practices to quiet the mind and cultivate inner serenity. Pursue avenues for personal growth and self-enhancement through continual learning and bible study. Surround yourself with a supportive faith based community or who offer guidance and encouragement. Adopt a daily gratitude practice to cultivate a positive outlook and acknowledge life's blessings. By consistently dedicating time and energy to your spiritual well-being, you can perpetuate the inner peace and growth achieved through spiritual life coaching.

Additional Resources for Spiritual Development: To augment your spiritual development and perpetuate your journey of self-discovery, an array of additional resources is available. These resources complement your spiritual life coaching experience, providing further direction and inspiration.

Explore the following resources:

- Books and literature on Christian spirituality, personal development, and mindfulness.
- Online courses or workshops delving deeper into specific biblical spiritual themes or practices.
- Local faith based communities or congregations offering opportunities for camaraderie and shared spiritual exploration.

By leveraging these supplementary resources, you can extend your spiritual growth beyond the confines of spiritual life coaching, embarking on a lifelong expedition of personal metamorphosis.

As you integrate the insights and wisdom gleaned from spiritual life coaching, acknowledge that your spiritual journey is singular to you. Embrace the process, remain receptive to novel experiences, and trust in your inner wisdom as you move on the path toward biblical based spiritual fulfillment and inner harmony.

The Potential for Personal Growth

Embarking on a healing journey holds the promise of significant personal growth. By addressing past hurts and challenging limiting beliefs, individuals can cultivate heightened self-awareness, inner strength, and resilience. This transformative process involves learning new coping strategies and fostering a positive mindset, contributing to an enhanced sense of well-being and an improved overall quality of life.

Healing from Within: The Power of Self-Healing

Inner healing is a self-discovery journey that necessitates reflection and a willingness to confront emotions and thoughts. A potent tool for this inner healing is self-healing, which involves utilizing our own inner resources to address physical, emotional, and spiritual aspects. This entails taking responsibility for well-being and employing prayer coupled with meditation, visualization, and biblical healing techniques to facilitate internal healing.

Engaging in self-healing practices connects individuals with their innate wisdom and the Holy Spirit. Through these methods, negative emotions can be released, past traumas can be addressed, and self-love and self-acceptance can be cultivated.

It's essential to note that while self-healing is valuable, it should not replace professional help when needed. Rather, it can serve as a powerful complement to traditional therapies, enhancing daily routines and fostering a deeper sense of inner peace and balance.

Healing the Mind: Unlocking Mental Well-being

Prioritizing mental health is integral to leading a fulfilling life. Inner healing plays a crucial role in unlocking mental well-being and fostering a positive mindset. Addressing negative thought patterns is a potent strategy, as thoughts significantly influence emotions and behavior. Identifying and challenging these patterns can shift perspectives, promoting positivity.

Effective stress management is also vital for mental well-being. Inner healing practices like prayer, mindfulness, and deep breathing can alleviate stress and promote relaxation. By nurturing the mind, individuals can develop a positive and resilient mindset, enabling them to navigate life's challenges with greater ease and confidence.

Healing the Past: Letting Go and Moving On

Healing the past is fundamental to inner healing, as holding onto past hurts and negative experiences can impede personal progress. Letting go is a process requiring patience, self-compassion, and a willingness to confront and heal from past wounds.

Forgiveness is a powerful tool for releasing the grip of the past. Though challenging, forgiving ourselves and others can be liberating, freeing space for healing and growth. Managing negative emotions is also crucial. Unresolved feelings such as anger, grief, and resentment can hinder progress, emphasizing the importance of developing healthy coping mechanisms to build resilience.

Healing Trauma: Reclaiming Your Inner Strength

Healing trauma is a critical component of the inner healing journey, acknowledging its profound impact on emotional and mental well-being. Proper healing involves acknowledging and validating the experience, seeking professional help, and employing techniques such as mindfulness to manage anxiety and stress associated with trauma.

It's crucial to seek support and guidance from mental health professionals, recognizing that healing from trauma is a time-consuming process. Practicing self-care and giving oneself the necessary time and space are essential components of this journey.

In conclusion, embracing inner healing is a transformative choice that can reshape one's life. By acknowledging emotions and investing in spiritual and emotional health, individuals can attain a state of inner peace and happiness, fostering personal growth and positive change.

The Process of Assisting Others in Healing

Establish Trust: Building a relationship of trust is foundational. This involves active listening, empathy, and a non-judgmental approach. Proverbs 11:13 praises a trustworthy spirit, and creating a safe space for individuals to open up is critical.

Identify the Knots: Help the individual identify the knots in their lives, whether they are patterns of sin, emotional wounds, or unhealthy behaviors. This step requires discernment and gentle guidance to bring these issues to light without causing shame or further harm.

Encourage Personal Reflection: Encourage the individual to engage in reflective practices, perhaps providing questions or scripture passages to guide their meditation and prayer. The aim is to help them connect deeply with themselves and with God to understand the roots of their struggles.

Provide Biblical Guidance: Offer biblical wisdom and teachings that pertain to their specific knots. This could involve discussing scriptures on forgiveness, identity in Christ, or the power of the Holy Spirit to break chains of bondage.

Pray Together: Engage in prayer with and for the individual. This is not just a closing ritual but a powerful tool for invoking God's intervention and comfort. Ephesians 6:18 urges us to pray on all occasions with all kinds of prayers and requests.

Offer Practical Steps: Provide actionable steps they can take, which may include seeking forgiveness, making amends, setting healthy boundaries, or pursuing counseling or pastoral care. James 2:17 reminds us that faith without deeds is dead, so practical application is essential.

Follow-Up: Be available for ongoing support. The process of untangling knots is rarely a one-time event but a journey that requires perseverance. Regular check-ins can provide the accountability and encouragement needed to sustain progress.

Celebrate Progress

Celebrating each triumph, no matter its size, is vital to bolstering an individual's confidence and sustaining their motivation on their journey to wholeness. In line with 1 Thessalonians 5:11, "Therefore encourage one another and build each other up, just as in fact you are doing," we are reminded of the importance of mutual upliftment and positive reinforcement. By recognizing and rejoicing in every step of progress, we affirm the individual's efforts and inspire continued perseverance towards healing and self-discovery.

In conclusion, aiding others in unraveling their life's intricate knots can be evangelistic mission, requiring individuals who are prayerful, patient, and compassionate, and who have walked the road of transformation.

These helpers are not merely guides but living embodiments of God's redemptive might, vessels for His love and wisdom to mend the brokenhearted and liberate the bound, thereby carrying out Christ's healing work on earth.

The concept of indulging in self-pampering as a means of continual advancement represents a burgeoning movement, where acknowledging your achievements serves as a catalyst for personal growth. Allocating time for oneself, engaging in self-reflection, and shifting focus from self-critique to self-applause fosters joy and contentment.

Granting oneself credit for progress, irrespective of its magnitude, is imperative. Recognizing hurdles surmounted and beneficial changes instigated is paramount. Commemorating progress not only engenders fulfillment and self-assurance but also ignites motivation.

Amidst life's frenetic pace, it's vital to pause and acknowledge the personal strides made and the distance covered. Every stride forward, regardless of its size, epitomizes resilience and dedication to self-improvement. Reflecting on conquered obstacles, imbibed lessons, and positive transformations is essential.

By embracing and reveling in one's progress, a sense of fulfillment, self-assurance, and impetus to continue the journey are nurtured. Additionally, it's important to acknowledge and honor the accomplishments of others.

Supporting one another contributes to the cultivation of a positive and nurturing community where everyone can flourish. Take the time to recognize and celebrate the achievements and personal growth of those around you.

Expressing appreciation and offering support for others' journeys not only uplifts them but also fosters a culture of positivity and encouragement. By acknowledging the successes of others, you contribute to an atmosphere of celebration and empowerment, creating a space where everyone can thrive and embrace their individual paths.

Amidst the busyness of life, remember to carve out moments of quietude for yourself. Even when your schedule feels overloaded, prioritize self-care and solitude. These precious moments of tranquility provide an opportunity to recharge, reflect, and reconnect with your inner self.

Use this time to pamper yourself and engage in activities that bring you joy and relaxation. Whether indulging in hobbies, praying, reading, or simply enjoying a leisurely bath, prioritize self-care practices that nourish your mind, body, and spirit. By dedicating time to you, you can experience the rejuvenating benefits of self-care and cultivate a greater sense of well-being.

Instead of dwelling on your perceived shortcomings, it's essential to acknowledge and celebrate your progress. Rather than criticizing yourself for areas where you may feel lacking, redirect your focus towards appreciating how far you've come. Reflect on your growth, the valuable lessons learned, and the positive changes you've initiated in your life.

By shifting your mindset towards celebration and self-appreciation, you cultivate a nurturing and empowering outlook that fuels ongoing progress and instills a profound sense of self-worth.

Take time to express gratitude and commemorate the blessings, both significant and small, that enrich your life. Embracing abundance and recognizing the goodness inherent in your experiences, relationships, and accomplishments invites more positivity, joy, and fulfillment into your journey.

In embracing the delicate balance between self-care and celebration, it's crucial to acknowledge the abundance surrounding you. Cultivate an attitude of abundance, acknowledging the blessings that flow through your life.

As we embrace the practice of self-care and celebration, let's acknowledge the strides we've taken and nurture ourselves along the journey. By carving out moments of quiet reflection, recognizing the growth of others, shifting our focus towards celebration, and embracing the abundance present in our lives, we cultivate a life brimming with joy, gratitude, and self-love.

So pamper yourself, revel in your achievements, and take pride in your growth. Celebrate the remarkable journey you're on, and continue to shine brightly!

Reflections on Past Experiences

I'd like to share some personal stories about knots, which are unresolved memories that once affected how I perceived myself and others. The beauty of these stories is that I've managed to untangle these knots over time, allowing me to access joyful memories and develop greater confidence and compassion.

My Father Didn't Return

When I was a young child, my father left my mother and my siblings. I can't recall the exact day he left, but I remember the profound impact it had on my mother's demeanor. I became hyper-vigilant, constantly watching the long dirt road that served as the entrance to our community, hoping for his return.

One day, I saw a car approaching in a cloud of dust. Excitement surged through me, thinking it might be my father. I ran home as fast as I could, rushed inside, and exclaimed, "Hey Daddy!" The man in the room, however, was a stranger, and the disappointment on his face mirrored my own.

From that moment, I could never look at the plume of dust on the road in the same way. Unbeknownst to me, a knot had formed in my memory, which would remain unresolved for years. It hindered my ability to build and maintain a healthy, positive respect for men.

As a young adult, I made a covenant with myself never to abandon my family, a direct response to my father's actions. I realized that my own father's life choices were a lesson that many people fail to connect with. As a born-again believer and a minister promoting love and forgiveness, I felt compelled to release any resentment I held towards my father.

Over time, I sporadically communicated with my father, with our conversations being unmemorable. It wasn't until I attended my step-mother's funeral, at his request, that I truly confronted my unresolved emotions. Seeing him in person triggered anger, confusion, and pent-up emotions of rejection and shame because my father had never returned.

The blessing was that I spent a few days with him, starting the process of untangling the knots in my memory. It was a multi-layered journey, one that required patience and commitment.

The Stolen Candy

Another knot formed during my preteen years when I made a poor choice. I helped a family member carry groceries into their home and noticed a paper bag with candy. Temptation got the better of me, and I took the bag, indulging in the candy. Guilt quickly overcame me, and my brother, who refused to partake in my wrongdoing, exposed my actions.

My relative was understandably upset, as they bought the candy for their own children. This experience created another knot within me. I internalized my mistake and vowed never to hurt or disappoint anyone else. My vow, while positive, led me to seek excessive approval from others, and I became discouraged when I couldn't win or earn it.

Over time, I learned to forgive myself and reflect on the situation from a more mature perspective, realizing that I was just a child when I made that mistake.

My Favorite T-Shirt

As a teenager, I began working and buying my own clothing. I felt proud of my newfound independence. However, a knot formed when my brother wore my favorite t-shirt without asking and ruined it. I became irate and resented anyone who touched my belongings without permission.

Interestingly, this knot centered around that specific shirt as the reference point for the violation. My brother had gifted me nicer clothing and money, so my resentment was unfounded. It took time and situations with my wife, who occasionally used my possessions, for me to recognize the unresolved memory.

Acknowledging this knot allowed me to invite my wife to help me untangle it by sharing my story and asking her to seek my permission before using some of my belongings.

"You Sound Like a Country Singer"

When I was around 13 years old, I loved music and attempted to sang often. However, a relative told me that I sounded like a country singer. At the time, this felt like a negative remark, as I wanted to emulate gospel, blues, or R&B singers. This comment created a knot within me, leading me to hide my talent and refrain from sharing my songs with others.

At age 18, I decided to share my music again, but I needed to confront the person who made that comment and express how it had affected me. They were younger and less mature when they made the remark, so forgiveness was essential. I eventually resolved this knot, and it allowed me to accept feedback without seeking validation.

Broken Promise

After getting married, my wife and I worked hard to buy our first home, but things changed after the birth of our third child. My wife had to quit her job to care for the children, and we struggled to maintain our lifestyle on a single income, resulting in the foreclosure of our home. I blamed her silently for the forced changes, but I couldn't communicate my feelings, from fear of repeating a cycle, hence the commitment I made to not leave my family, as my father did.

Eventually, I opened up to my wife about my resentment, acknowledging that I had considered her actions a broken promise. We worked through the situation, realizing the important lessons it had taught us and the need for open communication in our marriage.

These knots in my memory serve as reminders of the importance of self-forgiveness, understanding, and effective communication in navigating life's challenges. Untangling them has allowed me to grow and develop greater compassion for myself and others.

Steps towards Resolving Personal Knots

Let's delve into how I untangled each of these knots and worked to resolve the memories step by step:

My Father Didn't Return

Step 1: Acknowledgment and Awareness

I began by acknowledging the unresolved knot related to my father's abandonment and its impact on my perception of men. Recognizing this was crucial in the first step toward resolution.

Step 2: Self-Reflection and Understanding

As a young adult, I consciously reflected on the connection between my father's actions and my determination never to leave my own family. This understanding allowed me to empathize with both my father's struggles and my own reactions.

Step 3: Reconnection and Open Communication

I continued to maintain sporadic contact with my father, even though our conversations were initially unmemorable. The pivotal moment came when I attended my step-mother's funeral. Facing my father in person triggered intense emotions, but it also allowed for an opportunity to communicate openly about my feelings.

Step 4: Forgiveness and Healing

During the visit with my father, I chose to extend forgiveness and began the healing process. This was a pivotal step in untangling the knot. It helped me release pent-up emotions of rejection and shame that had lingered for years.

Step 5: Commitment to Ongoing Resolution

Recognizing that untangling such deep knots takes time and patience, I committed myself to the ongoing process of resolving these memories. This commitment to personal growth and understanding was vital.

The Stolen Candy

Step 1: Acknowledgment and Acceptance of Responsibility

I started by acknowledging my role in taking the candy and accepting responsibility for my actions. This step was essential to recognize the knot's existence.

Step 2: Self-Forgiveness

I began forgiving myself for my past mistakes. Understanding that I was just a child when I made this choice allowed me to let go of self-blame.

Step 3: Learning from the Experience

I realized that the candy incident taught me valuable lessons about the consequences of my actions and the importance of empathy. I used this knowledge to grow as an individual.

My Favorite T-Shirt

Step 1: Identifying the Trigger

I identified that the trigger for this knot was the specific T-shirt that my brother had worn without asking. Recognizing the trigger was essential to understand the unresolved memory.

Step 2: Communicating with My Partner

I opened up to my wife about this knot and how it affected me. Sharing my story and my feelings allowed her to understand my perspective and support me in resolving it.

Step 3: Requesting Support and Understanding

I asked my wife for her help in untangling the knot by requesting her to seek my permission before using our belongings. Her support and understanding were crucial in this process.

"You Sound Like a Country Singer"

Step 1: Reconnecting with My Talent

I decided to reconnect with my passion for music and sharing my songs with others. This step required courage and a willingness to embrace my talent despite past criticism.

Step 2: Confronting the Source

I approached the relative who had made the comment about sounding like a country singer. I expressed how their words had affected me and shared my growth as an artist.

Step 3: Forgiving and Letting Go

Recognizing that the person had made the comment from a less mature perspective, I forgave them. This allowed me to let go of any lingering resentment and judgment.

Broken Promise

Step 1: Identifying the Cause of Resentment

I recognized that my resentment toward my wife stemmed from her quitting her job, which led to financial difficulties and the loss of our first home.

Step 2: Open Communication

I initiated open and honest communication with my wife, sharing my feelings and acknowledging that I had considered her actions a broken promise.

Step 3: Understanding and Growth

Through our discussions, we both gained a deeper understanding of the situation and the lessons it had taught us. This understanding allowed us to move forward and grow together as a couple.

The key steps in each of these cases involves acknowledgment, self-forgiveness, open communication, and a commitment to ongoing growth and resolution. These steps allowed me to gradually untangle the knots and find greater peace and understanding in my life.

Behavioral Patterns That Hinder Growth

Next, we will look at 'common knots' that I have seen. I also want to encourage the seeking of support, as untangling the knots of our internal struggles requires both self-awareness and divine guidance. These knots, such as people-pleasing, perfectionism, low self-esteem, anger, addiction, codependency, cynicism, and self-rejection, often manifest as habitual behaviors that can hinder our personal and spiritual growth.

People Pleasing

People pleasing often lead one to neglect personal needs in favor of seeking approval from others. Reflecting on such tendencies, one can seek God's affirmation instead, understanding that His acceptance is paramount and unwavering.

If you find yourself constantly striving to please others at the expense of your own well-being, you may identify with the term "people-pleaser." While being kind and helpful is generally admirable, excessively prioritizing others' needs can lead to emotional exhaustion, stress, and anxiety.

People-pleasers often place others' needs above their own and may struggle to advocate for themselves. This tendency can stem from a personality trait known as "sociotropy," where individuals are overly concerned with earning approval to maintain relationships.

However, chronic people-pleasing can have detrimental effects, both on individuals and those around them:

Stress: Constantly over-committing and neglecting personal needs can lead to feelings of stress and overwhelm.

Fatigue: Taking on too much or adopting an inauthentic persona to please others can be mentally and physically draining.

Neglect: Prioritizing others may result in neglecting one's own self-care, including hygiene, health, and personal development.

Resentment: People-pleasers may harbor feelings of resentment towards those they constantly cater to, leading to passive-aggressive behavior and relationship strain.

Loss of identity: Excessive focus on pleasing others can cause individuals to lose sight of their own desires and values, leading to a diminished sense of self.

Breaking the cycle of people-pleasing requires self-awareness and intentional effort. Some strategies to consider include:

Starting small: Begin by setting boundaries and meeting your own needs gradually.

Stalling: Give yourself time to consider requests before responding impulsively.

Setting time limits: Establish boundaries by placing time constraints on commitments.

Time blocking: Allocate dedicated time for self-care and prioritize personal needs.

Rehearsing "no": Practice assertive communication and learn to decline requests gracefully.

Changing people-pleasing behavior may require professional support, particularly if it's rooted in underlying mental health conditions like Dependent Personality Disorder (DPD). Therapy can help individuals identify harmful patterns, set healthy boundaries, and regain a sense of self-worth.

Remember, it's okay to prioritize your own well-being and set boundaries in relationships. By cultivating self-awareness and embracing self-care, you can break free from the cycle of people-pleasing and lead a more fulfilling life.

Perfectionism

Perfectionism sets impossibly high standards, causing constant feelings of failure. Through reflection, one can learn to accept human limitations and embrace God's grace, which covers our imperfections.

Here's what perfectionism may be costing you:

Your Time and Money: Perfectionism often leads to excessive time and resource consumption. Constantly striving for flawlessness can result in spending more time than necessary on tasks or projects. Additionally, procrastination, a common coping mechanism for perfectionists, wastes valuable time before starting tasks.

Your Self-esteem: Perfectionism can contribute to low self-esteem as individuals hold themselves to unrealistically high standards. Perceiving mistakes as personal failures and engaging in negative self-talk can erode self-confidence.

Your Creativity: The pursuit of perfection stifles creativity by instilling fear of failure and reluctance to share ideas. Perfectionists may dismiss creative ideas as insignificant or overly critical of their own work, hindering the creative process.

Your Health: Demanding perfection from oneself can lead to mental stress, anxiety, and depression. Physical health may also be compromised due to stress-related issues and overexertion in pursuit of flawless outcomes.

Your Relationships: Perfectionists may struggle to maintain healthy relationships due to unrealistic expectations and difficulty showing compassion towards themselves and others. Projecting fears and standards onto others can create tension and strain in relationships.

Your Joy: Constantly striving for perfection can detract from the enjoyment of the process. Fear of not achieving flawless outcomes can overshadow the journey towards success, making it challenging to find joy and fulfillment in the pursuit of goals.

Perfectionism can hinder personal growth, creativity, well-being, and relationships if left unchecked. It's important to recognize that perfection is unattainable and that doing one's best is sufficient. Embracing imperfection and valuing progress over perfection can lead to greater happiness and fulfillment.

Low Self-Esteem

Low Self-Esteem can make us feel unworthy of love and success. Reflecting on God's words can help replace these thoughts with the truth that we are cherished and valued by Him.

Our self-image, or how we perceive ourselves, is largely shaped during our formative years of early childhood development. The relationship dynamics between children and their parents or caregivers play a pivotal role in this process. Feeling worthy and accepted, especially by those closest to us, is fundamental for developing a healthy self-image. Children inherently crave love and affirmation above all else.

However, even well-intentioned parents can sometimes fall short in providing the necessary love and validation their children need. Dysfunctional parent-child relationships can further exacerbate this issue, leading to millions of individuals worldwide harboring negative perceptions of their self-worth.

When our fundamental needs for love and affection aren't met during childhood, we run the risk of carrying poor self-image and low self-esteem into adolescence and adulthood. It's remarkable how many issues addressed in counseling sessions stem from unresolved childhood experiences.

It's crucial to understand that poor self-image is not innate but a learned belief. While some children may naturally be quiet or introverted, this doesn't necessarily equate to low self-esteem. Similarly, being quiet or introverted as an adult doesn't automatically imply low self-esteem, and it's essential to differentiate between inherent personality traits and learned beliefs about self-worth.

Unfortunately, many individuals may not take action to address their negative beliefs because they perceive them as intrinsic and unchangeable. These beliefs have been ingrained over many years, becoming deeply ingrained in their psyche and shaping their perception of reality. However, it's important to recognize that thoughts can become beliefs that influence behavior, and this cycle can perpetuate and validate negative self-beliefs.

Acknowledging and challenging these ingrained beliefs is the first step towards cultivating a healthier self-image. With self-awareness and intentional effort, individuals can work to reshape their beliefs about themselves and cultivate greater self-worth and confidence. Therapy and counseling can be valuable tools in this journey of self-discovery and personal growth.

The Bible serves as a reliable source for understanding our true identity, free from the biases of human perspective. A crucial initial step towards self-acceptance involves recognizing one's identity in Christ, acknowledging that we are created in God's image, and finding our worth rooted in Him, the source of genuine love and affirmation.

Navigating self-esteem within the Christian context can be challenging due to the emphasis on humility. Some interpret humility as self-denigration or devaluation, contrary to biblical teachings.

In response to a question from religious leaders about the greatest commandment, Jesus emphasized the importance of loving God wholeheartedly and loving one's neighbor as oneself (Matthew 22:37-39). This implies that self-love is a prerequisite for loving others effectively.

As God encourages fellowship among believers, feelings of unworthiness, insecurity, and lack of confidence can hinder meaningful connections. Such negative self-perceptions can also impede the fulfillment of God-given purposes.

A biblical perspective on self-love forms the foundation for self-acceptance. It entails acknowledging one's weaknesses and imperfections without diminishing self-worth. Achieving a balanced view involves recognizing shortcomings and strengths, sins and virtues, failures and achievements.

Anger

Anger may be a protective response to deeper emotional wounds. Reflective practices can uncover these underlying issues and invite God's peace to heal and soothe past hurts.

Anger can play a complex role in the deepening of inner wounds. While it is a normal and natural emotion, prolonged or intense anger can contribute to the exacerbation of emotional pain. Here are several ways in which anger may deepen inner wounds:

Suppressed Emotions: When people suppress or deny their feelings of anger, they may internalize these emotions. Unexpressed anger can turn inward and contribute to resentment, bitterness, and self-blame, deepening emotional wounds.

Escalation of Conflict: Expressing anger inappropriately or in a destructive manner can escalate conflicts and lead to further emotional distress. If anger is not managed effectively, it can damage relationships and intensify existing wounds.

Negative Thought Patterns: Anger can fuel negative thought patterns, such as rumination and dwelling on past hurts. This continuous cycle of negative thinking can perpetuate emotional pain and prevent healing.

Physical Health Effects: Chronic anger is associated with various health issues, including increased stress levels, high blood pressure, and compromised immune function. The physical toll of anger can contribute to overall well-being and may hinder the healing process.

Reinforcement of Victimhood: If anger is used as a defense mechanism to cope with feelings of victimization, it can perpetuate a sense of helplessness and deepen wounds. This victim mindset may hinder personal growth and hinder the ability to move forward.

Impact on Mental Health: Persistent anger can contribute to the development or exacerbation of mental health conditions such as anxiety and depression. These conditions can further complicate the process of healing from inner wounds.

Interference with Coping Mechanisms: Individuals may use unhealthy coping mechanisms, such as substance abuse or aggressive behavior, to deal with their anger. These behaviors can contribute to a cycle of self-destructive patterns, hindering the ability to address and heal inner wounds.

It's important to recognize and manage anger in a healthy way to prevent it from deepening inner wounds. Seeking support from friends, family, or mental health professionals, practicing effective communication, and learning healthy coping mechanisms can contribute to emotional healing and growth.

Moreover addiction often serves as an escape from pain but leads to destructive patterns. Reflection can reveal the deeper emotional voids that one attempts to fill with substances or behaviors, allowing one to seek fulfillment and healing in God instead.

Codependency involves an excessive reliance on others for approval and a sense of identity. Reflecting on such dynamics within relationships can lead to a greater understanding of one's inherent worth in God's eyes, fostering independence and a healthy self-concept.

Cynicism, or pervasive negativity, which often arises from disillusionment with the world. Reflecting on cynicism against the backdrop of faith can open one up to the hope and redemption offered through a relationship with God.

Self-Rejection is rejecting one's own identity and worth, often due to past negative experiences. Through reflection, one can begin to see themselves through the lens of God's love, affirming that they are indeed worthy and accepted.

Reflective Practices to unravel the following Knots

For Codependency: Reflect on memories of relationships where dependence on the other person overshadowed personal growth. Seeking God's sufficiency is key to understanding that true worth and stability are derived from Him.

For Quick-to-Anger: Recall instances where small triggers led to significant anger. Seeking insight from the Holy Spirit about the root causes can lead to a transformation of these reactions into more peaceful responses.

For Overly Self-Critical: Consider moments of harsh self-judgment and invite God into these memories. Embracing His grace can transform self-criticism into self-compassion.

For Self-Rejection: Reflect on times of self-sabotage or rejection of personal achievements. Understanding God's view of you as precious and valuable can help heal this self-rejection and move you towards self-acceptance.

In conclusion, through reflection, we can untangle these knots by identifying and understanding the underlying causes of our behaviors. Pairing reflection with scripture can provide the wisdom and strength needed for transformation. As James 1:22 exhorts us to be doers of the word, engaging in reflective practices can lead to actionable change, aligning our lives more closely with the teachings of Christ and our true identity in Him. In reflection, let God speak to those moments, replacing self-condemnation with His grace and love.

Chapter 10:   Embracing Healing: Resolving Memories One at a Time

As we continue this journey of healing and begin the process of untangling the knots of our past, I want to encourage each of you to be patient and vulnerable to the leading of the Holy Spirit. Healing is not a linear path, and it often involves moments of forgiveness, self-reflection, and a deepening connection with God's guidance.

Integrating inner strength and mindful approaches is essential. Renowned Christian author C.S. Lewis once said: "Getting over a painful experience is much like crossing monkey bars. You have to let go at some point to move forward."

As you release the grip on past pain, you create space for emotional healing. Be mindful of the emotions that arise during this process, and allow yourself to experience them fully. Healing often involves acknowledging and embracing the pain before it can be released.

Patience and Vulnerability

Healing is a deeply personal and often gradual process. Some of you may be led to forgive others, and at times, even yourselves. This forgiveness is a powerful step towards liberation from the knots that bind you. However, it's important to recognize that healing can ebb and flow. There may be moments when you are drawn more deeply into the process, and other times when you may feel the urge to stop. In those moments of hesitation, I encourage you to be patient with yourselves.

Viewing vulnerability within the context of our journey towards healing reveals it as an emblem of courage and authenticity. However, rather than embracing bravery and vulnerability, our instincts often prioritize self-preservation. Society conditions us to perceive vulnerability as a liability, a state overflowing with emotions that render us feeble. Exposing our raw feelings, risking judgment or misunderstanding, is daunting. Yet, it is within this vulnerability that the seeds of healing are sown.

In a world where success is often synonymous with emotional detachment, expressing our true selves is viewed as weakness. Asserting our vulnerability can therefore be a liberating act. The healing process is seldom a grand spectacle; it unfolds quietly within the recesses of our minds and bodies.

Consider human connections: vulnerability unlocks deeper intimacy, enabling authentic connections. Through vulnerability, we unveil our true selves, fostering genuine relationships that underpin our healing journey. Sharing our fears, hopes, and heartaches allows others to empathize and support us.

Vulnerability also nurtures self-compassion, a vital component of healing. Acknowledging our weaknesses, mistakes, and insecurities fosters personal growth. By embracing our imperfections, we create a compassionate space for self-forgiveness, learning, and resilience.

Moreover, vulnerability fuels creativity and innovation. It encourages risk-taking and the exploration of new perspectives, facilitating novel solutions to challenges encountered along the healing journey.

Consider the relationship between vulnerability and courage. Though seemingly contradictory, they are deeply intertwined. Stepping into vulnerability demonstrates courage—the courage to reveal our true selves, to take risks, and to grow. This courage enhances resilience, furthering our healing.

Furthermore, vulnerability cultivates empathy, fostering connections rooted in shared understanding. By exposing our vulnerable sides, we create a space where empathy flourishes, connecting us on a deeper level.

Embracing vulnerability allows us to find joy in uncertainty, recognizing it as a gateway to infinite possibilities. This adaptability proves invaluable in managing adversities and navigating recovery.

Additionally, vulnerability facilitates self-discovery, prompting introspection and insight into our true selves. This self-awareness enables us to recognize emotional triggers, manage reactions, and identify healing needs.

Vulnerability is not merely a state of being but an active process requiring conscious effort. It dismantles barriers, enabling us to confront fears and insecurities with strength. Embracing vulnerability in the healing journey reveals it not as weakness, but as a testament to our strength, courage, and spirit. As we embrace vulnerability, we embark on a journey of healing, discovering our innate potential to thrive amidst life's challenges.

The Holy Spirit's Guidance

Just as it took years to accumulate the knots you now carry, the Holy Spirit is well-equipped to lead you through the process of unraveling them one by one. In Proverbs 3:5-

6, we find guidance: "Trust in the Lord with all your heart and lean not on your own understanding; in all your ways submit to him, and he will make your paths straight." Trust in God's guidance and timing, for He knows what's best for your healing journey.

To be "filled with the Spirit" refers to a continuous process of allowing oneself to be influenced, guided, and empowered by the Holy Spirit in the Christian faith. It signifies an ongoing relationship and cooperation with the Spirit of God, wherein one opens themselves to the presence and workings of the Holy Spirit in their life.

The guidance of the Holy Spirit is a precious aspect of our blessings in the kingdom. The world's cultural norms and religious teachings often emphasize independence, self-reliance, self-promotion, and control. However, this contradicts the essence of kingdom culture. Instead, scripture instructs us to place complete trust in God, to refrain from leaning on our own understanding, and to acknowledge Him in all aspects of our lives.

By doing so, we allow Jesus to lead us in every step of our journey. Nevertheless, transitioning from the ways we've been taught to function to aligning with how Jesus operates requires time, discipline, and a sincere desire to love Him as He loves us. Jesus exemplified this perfectly during His time on earth, stating that He only acted in accordance with His Father's will and spoke what He heard from His Father (John 5:19). We are called to allow the Holy Spirit, through God's Word, to mold us into His likeness until His return or until we join Him in Heaven (1 John 3:2).

Incorporating God into our daily decision-making process is akin to consulting a spouse about which car to purchase, where, and how much to pay for it. Since Jesus has provided us with every good thing, it is prudent to seek His guidance in managing our finances, raising our children, nurturing our marriages, and conducting our businesses. Entrusting the reins to Jesus and following His direction often leads to a significant reduction in stress and anxiety levels.

Furthermore, for many of us, spiritual growth necessitates inner healing. This healing occurs as we invite the Holy Spirit to illuminate areas in our hearts that require His touch. Through this process, the Lord directs us to the truths in His Word that facilitate restoration. Unhealed wounds or distorted perspectives can impede our growth and create a sense of stagnation. By actively opening our hearts to the Holy Spirit, especially when confronted with challenging situations or individuals, we undergo a transformation in our thought patterns, experiencing a renewal of our minds.

Guiding Principles for Positive Change

To help you navigate this process, consider the wisdom of Christian author Max Lucado, who reminds us: "Forgiveness is unlocking the door to set someone free and realizing you were the prisoner!" Forgiveness is not only a gift to others but a liberating force for your own healing.

Personal Growth through Inner Reflection

In Psalm 139:23-24, we are encouraged to pray: "Search me, O God, and know my heart; test me and know my thoughts! And see if there be any grievous way in me, and lead me in the way everlasting." Inner reflection and self-examination are essential components of personal growth. Allow God's light to shine on the areas that need healing.

In conclusion, as you resolve memories one at a time, remember that you are not alone on this journey. God's presence and guidance are with you, and there are timeless principles and wisdom from Christian authors to guide your way. Be patient, be vulnerable, and trust in the transformative power of God's healing grace. Each memory untangled is a step toward the freedom and wholeness you deserve.

Self-reflection serves as a foundational element of personal development, enabling individuals to glean profound insights into their thoughts, emotions, and behaviors. Through introspection, one can pinpoint recurring patterns that might impede their journey towards realizing their utmost potential.

Whether through journaling, prayer, or a tranquil stroll amidst nature, self-reflection furnishes a potent tool for attaining clarity and a broader perspective on life's intricacies. This process facilitates the establishment of objectives and the formulation of actionable strategies to manifest aspirations and evolve into the finest rendition of oneself.

What Constitutes Self-Reflection? At its core, self-reflection is a pivotal mechanism for personal evolution. It entails scrutinizing one's thoughts, emotions, and deeds to cultivate self-awareness and refine oneself. By dissecting past experiences, discerning their essence, and assimilating their lessons, individuals can discern their strengths and vulnerabilities, paving the way for a roadmap of self-improvement.

Moreover, self-reflection fosters heightened empathy and comprehension of others, along with sharpened decision-making prowess. Through this introspective journey, individuals gain invaluable insights into their inner workings, which can catalyze positive transformations in both personal and professional spheres.

Self-reflection emerges as a practice of profound significance in our lives. It offers a respite from the whirlwind of daily existence, affording us the opportunity to scrutinize our encounters, thoughts, sentiments, and actions. Through this introspective process, we attain a deeper comprehension of ourselves, discerning our behavioral tendencies and the underlying motivations that propel us forward.

This heightened level of self-awareness proves pivotal for personal evolution, empowering us to pinpoint areas necessitating refinement and devise strategies for constructive change. Moreover, self-reflection serves as a catalyst for enhancing emotional intelligence, fostering mindfulness, and fortifying self-esteem and resilience.

By engendering a greater awareness of our interactions with others and fostering a discerning perspective through the analysis of past experiences, self-reflection equips us with the tools to make informed decisions and navigate life's complexities more adeptly. Regular engagement in self-reflection fosters a fulfilling existence, facilitating personal growth and overall well-being.

The Advantages of Self-Reflection Embarking on a journey of self-reflection yields manifold benefits conducive to personal development. By scrutinizing our thoughts, emotions, and deeds, we cultivate a heightened self-awareness that enables us to discern our strengths and weaknesses.

With this newfound clarity, we can devise a roadmap for personal advancement, leveraging our strengths while addressing areas requiring enhancement. Furthermore, self-reflection nurtures emotional intelligence and mindfulness, fostering sharper decision-making abilities and imbuing life with greater satisfaction.

Consistent practice of self-reflection can alleviate stress by bestowing clarity upon life's challenges, thereby enhancing overall well-being.

The Role of Self-Reflection in Personal Growth Self-reflection serves as a cornerstone for personal growth, enabling individuals to assess their strengths and weaknesses, identify limiting behavioral patterns, and gain a deeper understanding of their values and aspirations.

This process engenders clarity and purpose, empowering individuals to chart a course toward fulfillment and achievement. Moreover, regular engagement in self-reflection enhances communication skills and fosters emotional intelligence, facilitating ongoing learning and development.

Ultimately, self-reflection propels individuals toward a more purposeful and enriching existence, characterized by heightened self-awareness and the continual pursuit of growth and improvement.

Step by Step guide: Untangling the Knots of Your Past

As we begin the process of untangling the knots of our past, I want to offer you a step-by-step guide to aid you in this transformative journey. Remember, you are not alone, and the Holy Spirit is your guide and companion in this process.

In Romans 8:14, Paul presents a pivotal verse regarding our journey toward becoming fulfilled and complete Christians. He asserts, 'For as many as are led by the Spirit of God, these are sons of God.' The verb tense employed here is the continuing present tense, indicating that those who are consistently led by the Spirit of God are the true children of God.

The term 'sons' connotes maturity, suggesting not infancy but adulthood. Although the initial step toward becoming God's children is the spiritual rebirth, as elucidated by Jesus in John 3, achieving maturity and completeness necessitates a continual reliance on the guidance of the Holy Spirit. Unfortunately, a significant number of Christians, despite being born again and baptized in the Holy Spirit, fail to progress in their journey of being led by the Spirit.

Consequently, they remain stunted in their spiritual growth, falling short of the complete transformation God desires for them. Paradoxically, some individuals who frequently invoke the Holy Spirit's name may lack a genuine understanding of how to be led by Him.

Baptism in the Holy Spirit is not a one-time event. The initiation of an enduring relationship with the Father, facilitated through the Son, and sustained by the Holy Spirit.

One factor contributing to the lack of maturity among Christians is a fundamental misunderstanding of what it means to receive the righteousness of Christ. This misunderstanding impedes their ability to allow the Holy Spirit to guide them effectively, as they often rely on alternative methods for direction.

The Bible delineates two distinct paths to achieving righteousness with God: through adherence to the law or through grace. However, it is crucial to recognize that these paths are mutually exclusive. Seeking righteousness through the law precludes obtaining it through grace, and vice versa. Despite the significance of this distinction, it appears that many believers overlook or downplay its importance.

Observationally, it seems that a considerable number of Christians attempt to blend elements of both approaches—relying partially on the law and partially on grace. However, this amalgamation reflects a lack of understanding of either concept. An appreciation of both law and grace is essential for cultivating a deeper relationship with God and allowing oneself to be guided by the Spirit.

The concept of law entails adherence to a set of rules, with righteousness attained through strict compliance. Conversely, grace is unearned and unachievable through human effort; any attempt to earn it negates its essence. Grace is received solely through faith, as Ephesians 2:8 elucidates: "For by grace you have been saved through faith, and that not of yourselves; it is the gift of God." Through faith, grace leads to righteousness. Hence, the choice between law and grace is pivotal for those seeking righteousness and spiritual maturity.

The Bible unequivocally advises against pursuing righteousness through the law, as it asserts that no one can achieve it in this manner. Understanding why necessitates an examination of the law's requirements. Crucially, righteousness under the law demands perfect adherence to its entirety, consistently. Merely adhering to some aspects of the law at certain times or all aspects at select times falls short of fulfilling its requirements for righteousness. Therefore, continuous compliance with the entire law is imperative for achieving righteousness through this avenue.

Paul's elucidation of this concept in his letter to the Galatians emphasizes the inherent limitations of relying on the works of the law. He asserts, "For as many as are of the works of the law are under the curse; for it is written, 'Cursed is everyone who does not continue in all things which are written in the book of the law, to do them'" (Galatians 3:10).

Similarly, James reinforces this perspective by highlighting the interconnectedness of the commandments, stating, "For whoever shall keep the whole law, and yet stumble [fail] in one point, he is guilty of all. For He who said, 'Do not commit adultery,' also said, 'Do not murder.' Now if you do not commit adultery, but you do murder, you have become a transgressor of the law" (James 2:10-11). Consequently, to receive the blessings and evade the curse, one must meticulously adhere to every aspect of the law at all times. Selective obedience to certain commandments while disregarding others renders the law ineffective in achieving righteousness.

The Bible consistently underscores the futility of human efforts to fulfill the entirety of the law. Romans 3:20 reinforces this notion, stating, "Therefore by the deeds of the law [the keeping of the law] no flesh will be justified in His sight, for by the law is the knowledge of sin." Paul emphasizes that no individual can attain righteousness in God's eyes through adherence to the law.

One might question, "Then what was the purpose of God giving the law of Moses?" It's essential to understand that the law was never intended to bestow righteousness upon individuals. Instead, it served multiple purposes, one of which was to illuminate humanity's need for salvation. Additionally, the law demonstrated our inability to save ourselves.

As articulated in Romans 7:5, "For when we were in the flesh [when we were controlled by our fleshly nature], the sinful passions which were aroused by the law were at work in our members to bear fruit to death." This passage reveals the startling reality that the law had the effect of stirring up sinful impulses within us. Paul further elaborated on this concept in 1 Corinthians 15:56, stating, "The strength of sin is the law."

Personal experience can provide insight into this phenomenon. For instance, during my confirmation in the Anglican church at fifteen, I recognized the need to improve myself. I diligently memorized catechism questions and answers, genuinely striving to become a better person.

However, paradoxically, my efforts to be virtuous seemed to accelerate my descent into wrongdoing. This perplexing outcome stemmed from the law's ability to provoke sinful tendencies within me, which I later learned to be the manifestation of the "old man," the rebellious nature of the flesh. Striving to do what is right in one's own strength eventually unveils the realization of one's inadequacy to uphold righteousness independently.

The more one endeavors, the less success is attained. Another purpose of the law was to serve as a precursor, foretelling the arrival of the Savior who could redeem us. Paul illustrated this purpose when he wrote, "The law was our tutor to bring us to Christ, that we might be justified by faith" (Galatians 3:24). The term "tutor" translates to paidagogos in Greek, from which we derive the word pedagogue.

Originally, it referred to a senior slave in a wealthy household entrusted with the early education of children. His duties included teaching them fundamental concepts such as the alphabet, obedience, and distinguishing right from wrong. Additionally, he guided them through the streets to the actual school and its teacher once they outgrew his instruction. Similarly, the law imparts foundational principles of righteousness but ultimately directs us to Christ, the true lesson.

In Galatians 2:16, Paul underscored this truth, stating, "Knowing that a man is not justified by the works of the law" (emphasis added). The crucial question, therefore, is whether we genuinely grasp this concept—that righteousness is not attained through adherence to the law but through faith in Jesus Christ. As reiterated in Galatians 2:16, "even we have believed in Christ Jesus, that we may be justified by faith in Christ and not by the works of the law; for by the works of the law no flesh shall be justified." Our belief in Christ enables us to be righteous through faith in Him, rather than through strict adherence to the law's requirements.

Paul emphasized, "That no one is justified by the law in the sight of God is evident, for 'the just shall live by faith'" (Galatians 3:11). Living in faith serves as the alternative to living by the law, with these two approaches being mutually exclusive. Only through living in faith can we entrust the Holy Spirit to guide us and allow Him to lead our lives.

However, it appears from my observations that many Christians are not living in faith but instead exist in a state of ambiguity, caught between adherence to the law and reliance on grace. Unfortunately, this often results in experiencing the drawbacks of both approaches. Nonetheless, the truth remains that we have been liberated from the dominion of the law through Jesus' death, granting us the freedom to be led by the Spirit.

Paul elaborated on this liberation in Romans 7:4, stating, "Therefore, my brethren, you also have become dead to the law through the body of Christ, that you may be married to another; to Him who was raised from the dead, that we should bear fruit to God." Paul likened the relationship with the law to a marriage contract that binds individuals to their fleshly nature. Despite our efforts to uphold the law, we invariably fail due to the rebellious nature within us. However, the good news is that through Jesus' death on the cross, our fleshly nature was crucified with Him as Paul articulated, "Our old man was crucified with Him, that the body of sin might be done away with, that we should no longer be slaves of sin."

"For he who has died has been freed from sin" (Romans 6:6-7) through our death to what once held us (our fleshly nature), we have been liberated from the law, enabling us to serve in the newness of the Spirit rather than the oldness of the letter (Romans 7:6). While the law endures as part of God's eternal Word, Christ brought an end to its role in achieving righteousness.

As stated in Romans 10:4, "For Christ is the end of the law for righteousness to everyone who believes." Now that our fleshly nature has been put to death, we are free to enter into a new union with the resurrected Christ through the Spirit. This union produces the fruit of His righteousness, the fruit of the Spirit, in contrast to the offspring of the flesh that we bore when married to our fleshly nature. Consequently, our way of life is determined not by our efforts but by our union with Christ.

This encapsulates the essence of the Christian message. Mere attempts to be good and do what is right fall short of grasping this message fully. However, when we are united with Christ and live in that unity, we can be led by the Spirit.

The Protocol of Entering into Self-Deliverance

Entering into self-deliverance is a profound and deeply personal journey towards healing and spiritual freedom. It's a process that requires patience, faith, and an open heart to the leading of the Holy Spirit. Here, we will explore a protocol that can serve as a guide for those embarking on this transformative path.

Acknowledge the Need for Deliverance:

Acknowledging the need for deliverance is a pivotal step on the journey towards self-awareness and inner healing. It involves a deep recognition of the presence of internal struggles, whether they manifest as emotional wounds, psychological barriers, or patterns of behavior that hinder personal growth and fulfillment.

This acknowledgment often arises through various channels, such as introspection, prayer, or seeking guidance from wise and trusted mentors. Self-reflection allows individuals to delve into their inner landscape, exploring their thoughts, emotions, and experiences to identify areas of distress or stagnation. Prayer can serve as a means of connecting with God to seek clarity and guidance in understanding and addressing their internal struggles. Additionally, seeking counsel from trusted mentors, such as therapists, spiritual leaders, or wise friends, can provide valuable insight and support in navigating the complexities of one's inner world.

Recognizing the existence of internal knots, wounds, or strongholds is not an admission of weakness but rather a courageous acknowledgment of one's humanity and the complexities of the human experience. It signifies a willingness to confront and address the obstacles that stand in the way of personal growth, healing, and fulfillment. By acknowledging the need for deliverance, individuals take the first step towards reclaiming agency over their lives, empowering themselves to embark on a journey of self-discovery, healing, and transformation.

Seek God's Guidance and Protection:

It involves turning to God for support, wisdom, and divine intervention as one navigates the complexities of inner healing and transformation.

At the core of this step is heartfelt prayer—a sincere and earnest communication with the divine. Through prayer, individuals seek to establish a connection with God, inviting the presence of the Holy Spirit to guide and illuminate their path. This act of surrendering to God acknowledges human limitations and the need for divine intervention in the process of healing and deliverance.

In prayer, individuals may express their vulnerabilities, fears, and desires for healing, inviting God to intervene in their lives and reveal any areas in need of transformation. They may also seek divine protection from spiritual forces that may seek to hinder their progress or sabotage their efforts towards growth and healing.

Additionally, seeking God's guidance through prayer can provide clarity and discernment in navigating the complexities of inner turmoil and identifying the root causes of internal struggles. The Holy Spirit, believed by many to be a source of wisdom and insight, can illuminate hidden wounds, patterns of thought, and behaviors that may be contributing to one's suffering.

Ultimately, seeking God's guidance and protection before engaging in the process of self-deliverance is an act of faith and trust in him. It serves as a foundation for the journey ahead, providing strength, clarity, and divine support as individuals confront their inner demons and strive towards wholeness and healing.

Identify Specific Knots:

Identify and name the specific knots or issues you wish to address. This clarity will help you focus your prayers and intentions during self-deliverance.

Here's how you can go about identifying and naming these specific knots:

Reflect on your experiences: Take time to reflect on your life experiences, emotions, and patterns of behavior. Consider areas where you consistently encounter challenges, conflicts, or emotional distress. These could be recurring themes such as fear, anger, guilt, shame, or self-doubt.

Journaling: Writing down your thoughts, feelings, and experiences can be a powerful tool for self-reflection. Use journaling to explore your inner landscape, uncovering underlying beliefs, traumas, or unresolved issues that may be contributing to your distress.

Seek feedback: Reach out to trusted friends, family members, or mentors for feedback and perspective. Sometimes, others can offer insights into our blind spots or patterns of behavior that we may not be aware of ourselves.

Therapeutic techniques: If you're comfortable, consider exploring therapeutic techniques such as cognitive-behavioral therapy (CBT), mindfulness practices, or inner child work. These techniques can help you uncover subconscious beliefs, traumas, or emotional wounds that may be holding you back.

Prayer and meditation: Engage in prayer and meditation to seek guidance from God. Ask for clarity and insight into the specific knots or issues that need to be addressed during the self-deliverance process. Trust in the divine wisdom to reveal what needs healing and transformation within you.

Self-awareness exercises: Practice mindfulness and self-awareness exercises to become more attuned to your thoughts, emotions, and bodily sensations. Pay attention to any recurring patterns, triggers, or areas of discomfort that arise during your daily life.

Once you have identified and named the specific knots or issues you wish to address, you can then focus your prayers, intentions, and efforts during the self-deliverance process. This clarity enables you to target your healing journey more effectively, working towards untangling and releasing the internal struggles that are holding you back from living a life of wholeness and freedom.

Repentance and Forgiveness:

Healing often involves moments of repentance and forgiveness. Acknowledge any sins, mistakes, or bitterness in your heart, and ask for God's forgiveness. Extend forgiveness to those who have hurt or wronged you, releasing the power of these knots.

In your self-deliverance journey, incorporating these practices is pivotal for spiritual and emotional growth. Begin by courageously acknowledging any sins or mistakes, engaging in sincere self-reflection to identify areas where values may have been compromised or others inadvertently harmed. Taking this honest inventory requires humility and a commitment to recognizing personal shortcomings, approaching God with a contrite heart, confessing sins and seeking forgiveness. Trust in His mercy and grace to cleanse you of transgressions, fostering a sense of renewal.

Release the emotional burdens of bitterness, resentment, and anger that may have taken root within. Recognize these negative emotions as entangling knots, choosing the liberating path of forgiveness. Extend this gift to both yourself and others, regardless of their acknowledgment or change in behavior. Forgiveness becomes a powerful tool for personal liberation, allowing you to break free from the shackles of resentment and move forward with a lighter heart.

In prayer, surrender grievances to God, entrusting Him with the healing process. Allow His love and grace to permeate your heart, dissolving the knots of unforgiveness. While forgiveness is a personal decision, commit to reconciliation where appropriate and feasible. Rebuilding trust and repairing relationships may be a separate yet vital process guided by humility, empathy, and a dedication to healing.

Embracing repentance and forgiveness opens the door to the transformative power of grace and compassion. Through these practices, you can untangle the knots of guilt, shame, and resentment, allowing the radiant light of God's love to shine through and illuminate your path towards inner healing, wholeness, and reconciliation.

Use Scripture and Declarations:

The Word of God is a powerful tool in self-deliverance. Find relevant scriptures that speak to your specific issues and declare them aloud. Allow God's truth to replace the lies and negative patterns within you.

In the process of self-deliverance, integrating scripture and declarations can be a potent and transformative practice:

Begin by diligently searching the Bible for scriptures that directly address the specific challenges or entanglements you aim to overcome. For instance, if fear is a prevailing issue, turn to verses such as 2 Timothy 1:7 or Psalm 34:4 that speak to the liberation from fear through divine power.

Personalize the scriptures you've unearthed, adapting them to resonate with your unique situation, and craft declarations that affirm these personalized scriptures, making them a powerful and intimate proclamation of your faith. For instance, declare boldly, "I proclaim that God has not bestowed upon me a spirit of fear, but one of power, love, and a sound mind. I am liberated from fear and anxiety, for God's unwavering presence is with me."

Give voice to these declarations, speaking them aloud with conviction and faith. The spoken word possesses a profound impact on the psyche and spirit, reinforcing the truths found in God's word and dispelling falsehoods and negative thought patterns.

Integrate these declarations into your daily routine, repeating them consistently as a fundamental aspect of your self-deliverance practice. Consistent repetition plays a crucial role in reshaping thought patterns and aligning your beliefs with the profound truths embedded in God's word over time.

Combine these declarations with prayer, inviting the Holy Spirit to actively work within you, providing the strength, wisdom, and guidance needed to overcome your struggles. In your prayers, seek God's transformative power to align your heart and mind with His truth.

Above all, trust wholeheartedly in the promises of God's word. Embrace the understanding that His scripture holds unparalleled efficacy in bringing about transformation and deliverance in your life. Anchor your faith in His unwavering faithfulness, confident that as you persistently declare His promises, He will bring profound healing and deliverance on your self-discovery journey.

Renounce Strongholds:

Speak out loud your renunciation of any strongholds or negative patterns in your life. Renounce ties to any spiritual or generational influences contributing to your knots. Declare your allegiance to Christ. Here's how you can verbally renounce strongholds and declare your allegiance to Christ:

Identify specific strongholds: Reflect on areas of your life where you feel bound or held captive by negative patterns, behaviors, or influences. These could include addictions, harmful thought patterns, unhealthy relationships, or spiritual oppression.

Verbal renunciation: Speak out loud your renunciation of these strongholds, declaring your intention to break free from their grip. For example, you might say, "In the name of Jesus, I renounce the stronghold of addiction in my life. I declare that I am no longer bound by its power, and I choose to walk in freedom and victory."

Address spiritual and generational influences: Acknowledge any spiritual or generational influences that may be contributing to the strongholds in your life. Renounce ties to these influences, declaring your allegiance to Christ and His authority over your life. You could say, "I renounce any ties to spiritual influences that have sought to oppress me. I declare my allegiance to Christ and His lordship over every area of my life."

Affirm your identity in Christ: Declare your identity as a beloved child of God, redeemed and set free by the blood of Jesus. Affirm your position as an heir to the promises of God and a vessel of His love and grace. You might say, "I am a child of God, redeemed by the blood of Jesus. I am clothed in His righteousness, and I walk in His victory."

Pray for strength and guidance: Ask God for strength and guidance as you continue on your journey of deliverance and transformation. Invite the Holy Spirit to empower you to resist temptation, overcome obstacles, and walk in obedience to God's will.

Stay vigilant and persistent: Recognize that renouncing strongholds is often an ongoing process that requires vigilance and persistence. Stay committed to your declaration of freedom, relying on God's strength and grace to sustain you each step of the way.

By verbally renouncing strongholds and declaring your allegiance to Christ, you affirm your commitment to walk in freedom and victory as a child of God. Trust in His power to break every chain and lead you into a life of abundant joy, peace, and purpose.

Bind and Cast Out:

In the name of Jesus, bind the forces of darkness that may be influencing your knots. Command these negative influences to leave your life. Trust in the authority you have through Christ's name.

Incorporating the practice of invoking the name of Jesus into your self-deliverance process is a powerful and transformative approach:

Commence by acknowledging the unparalleled authority and power vested in the name of Jesus Christ. Understand that His name stands supreme, surpassing every other name, demons and negative forces must yield to His divine authority.

Discern any negative influences, spiritual strongholds, or oppressive forces that may be exerting their impact on your life. This could encompass spiritual attacks, demonic oppression, or entrenched patterns of sin and bondage.

With unwavering confidence and faith, speak out loud as you bind these negative influences in the mighty name of Jesus. Affirm your authority as a believer and command these forces to vacate your life. For instance, boldly declare, "In the name of Jesus, I bind every spirit of fear, addiction, and oppression that is operating in my life. I command you to leave me now and go where Jesus sends you."

Place your trust in the authority of Jesus Christ to enforce your commands and triumph over every force of darkness. Rely on His strength and power as you exercise your authority as a cherished child of God.

In your prayers, beseech God for protection and cleansing. Ask Him to envelop you in His protective presence and to purify you from any lingering influences or residues of darkness. Open yourself to the Holy Spirit, inviting Him to fill you anew with His empowering presence for spiritual warfare.

Maintain a posture of continual prayer and vigilance, recognizing that the adversary may attempt to return or retaliate. Ground yourself in God's word, persist in seeking His guidance, and hold firm to His promise of never leaving or forsaking you.

By binding and casting out negative influences in the name of Jesus, you not only assert your authority as a believer but also invite the intervention of God's mighty power in your life. Trust wholeheartedly in His faithfulness to protect, deliver, and bring about transformation according to His perfect will.

Seek Support and Accountability:

Self-deliverance can be an intense and emotional process. Don't hesitate to seek support from trusted friends, family members, or spiritual mentors who can pray with you, offer guidance, and hold you accountable.

Incorporating trusted individuals into your self-deliverance journey can significantly enhance your support system and overall experience:

Start by identifying a support network composed of friends, family members, or spiritual mentors whom you trust implicitly and with whom you feel comfortable confiding. Select individuals who will offer unconditional support and compassionate understanding.

Openly share your self-deliverance journey with your support network, unveiling the struggles, challenges, and aspirations that define your path. Foster an environment of honesty and transparency, allowing these trusted individuals to walk alongside you with empathy and support.

Initiate prayer sessions both individually and collectively with your support network. Seek divine guidance, strength, and protection as you navigate the intricacies of self-deliverance, inviting your loved ones to join you in prayer and intercession.

Rely on your support network for guidance and accountability in adhering to your self-deliverance goals. Share your progress, setbacks, and triumphs with them, allowing their presence to act as a source of encouragement and a reminder of your commitments.

Welcome words of encouragement, affirmation, and motivation from your support network, particularly during challenging moments. Embrace the reassurance that you are not traversing this journey alone, finding strength in the collective support of those who care about your well-being.

Be open to receiving constructive feedback and insights from your support network, even when it may be difficult to hear. Trust in the value of their perspectives, recognizing that their input can offer valuable guidance to help you grow and surmount obstacles.

Express genuine gratitude for the unwavering support and encouragement received from your network. Acknowledge their presence, prayers, and willingness to accompany you in your journey of self-deliverance. Together, celebrate victories and overcome challenges, fostering a sense of unity, faith, and love within your shared community.

Maintain a Lifestyle of Holiness:

Deliverance is not a one-time event but a continual process. Maintain a lifestyle of holiness, regularly seeking God's presence through prayer, worship, and studying His Word. Here are some key practices to incorporate into your life to cultivate holiness:

Regular prayer: Cultivate a consistent prayer life, setting aside time each day to commune with God, express gratitude, seek guidance, and intercede for yourself and others. Prayer is essential for nurturing your relationship with God and inviting His presence into every aspect of your life.

Devotional study: Dedicate time to studying and meditating on God's Word daily. Engage in devotional reading, Bible study, and reflection to deepen your understanding of Scripture and apply its teachings to your life. Allow God's Word to shape your thoughts, attitudes, and actions.

Worship: Make worship a central part of your life, both individually and corporately. Worship through music, prayer, and praise, expressing your love and adoration for God. Participate in congregational worship gatherings to connect with other believers and magnify God's name together.

Fellowship: Surround yourself with fellow believers who share your commitment to holiness and spiritual growth. Participate in the Christian community through small groups, church services, and fellowship activities, where you can encourage, support, and hold one another accountable in your faith journey.

Practicing obedience: Seek to live in obedience to God's commands and leading, aligning your thoughts, words, and actions with His will. Allow the Holy Spirit to convict and guide you in areas where you need to make adjustments or repentance and strive to walk in righteousness and integrity.

Spiritual disciplines: Incorporate spiritual disciplines such as fasting, solitude, and silence into your life to cultivate intimacy with God and deepen your spiritual awareness. These practices help to quiet the noise of the world and create space for God to speak and work in your life.

Accountability: Surround yourself with trusted individuals who can provide accountability and support in your journey of holiness. Be open to feedback and correction from others who have your best interests at heart, and humbly receive guidance and encouragement as needed.

By maintaining a lifestyle of holiness characterized by prayer, worship, studying God's Word, fellowship, obedience, spiritual disciplines, and accountability, you create a fertile environment for spiritual growth, transformation, and ongoing deliverance. Embrace this journey with perseverance and reliance on God's grace, knowing that He who began a good work in you will carry it to completion until the day of Christ Jesus (Philippians 1:6).

Reflect and Assess:

Periodically reflect on your journey of self-deliverance. Assess your progress, celebrate victories, and continue to address any new knots that may surface. Remember that healing is an ongoing journey.

In your ongoing journey of self-deliverance, incorporating reflection and assessment can be instrumental for sustained growth and transformation:

Establish regular moments for reflection, carving out dedicated time weekly or monthly for introspection. Create a serene environment free from distractions, allowing yourself to delve into deep self-assessment.

Celebrate the victories and breakthroughs encountered along the way. Acknowledge and revel in overcoming fears, breaking free from detrimental habits, or experiencing emotional healing. Each milestone serves as a testament to both your resilience and the faithfulness of God.

Conduct an honest evaluation of your progress in addressing the knots and issues initially identified in your self-deliverance journey. Reflect on areas where substantial growth has occurred and recognize any aspects that may still necessitate attention or deeper healing.

Stay attuned to your internal landscape during the reflection process and identify any new knots or challenges that may have emerged. Life is dynamic, and being proactive in addressing new concerns is essential for continued personal development.

Should new knots or challenges arise, seek guidance and support from trusted friends, mentors, or spiritual advisors. Share your reflections and concerns with them, drawing upon their wisdom and encouragement as you navigate the next steps in your journey.

Adjust your self-deliverance strategies based on your reflections and assessments. Consider incorporating new practices, exploring additional resources, or deepening your engagement with existing spiritual disciplines to address ongoing challenges and foster continuous growth.

Practice self-compassion throughout the reflection and assessment process. Recognize that healing is a journey with its share of setbacks and challenges. Offer yourself grace and kindness, understanding that each step forward brings you closer to the wholeness and freedom God desires for you.

By integrating regular reflection and assessment into your self-deliverance journey, you maintain momentum and experience healing and transformation. Embrace the understanding that healing is an ongoing process, and every forward stride brings you nearer to the wholeness and freedom that God envisions for your life.

Seeking Assistance from Others:

While self-deliverance can be a powerful and transformative process, there are times when seeking assistance from others is necessary. Recognizing when to seek help is pivotal in the self-deliverance journey. If the intensity of emotions, thoughts, or spiritual experiences becomes overwhelming, it's crucial to reach out to trusted friends, family members, or spiritual advisors who can offer support and guidance.

Persistent struggles or seemingly insurmountable obstacles may indicate the need for specialized assistance from professional counselors, therapists, or experienced mentors. Acknowledging the reality of spiritual warfare and enlisting the support of fellow believers can provide essential strength and solidarity against spiritual attacks. When encountering resistance during self-deliverance, surrounding yourself with a supportive community can offer encouragement and spiritual covering.

For deeply ingrained or complex issues, seeking assistance from professionals in areas such as trauma therapy or deliverance ministry can provide tailored support. Safety-related concerns, including domestic violence or severe mental health issues, should prompt immediate assistance from trained professionals. Embracing your limitations and asking for help demonstrates humility and a commitment to well-being and spiritual growth. Trust in the transformative power of community and relationships to bring healing and freedom in your life.

Here are some considerations for when to reach out for help:

Complex or Deep-Seated Issues: This refers to problems or challenges that are not easily resolved and may have deep roots in a person's psyche or spiritual life. Examples could include long-standing patterns of behavior, unresolved trauma, or deeply ingrained beliefs. In such cases, seeking guidance from someone with specialized training, such as a spiritual counselor or deliverance minister, can be beneficial. These individuals are trained to provide insights, techniques, and support tailored to addressing complex issues effectively.

Lack of Progress: Sometimes, despite our best efforts, we may find ourselves stuck in our journey towards spiritual or emotional healing. This could lead to frustration or even emotional distress. If self-help methods are not yielding the desired results, it's wise to seek assistance from those with more experience. This could involve consulting with individuals who have expertise in spiritual guidance or prayer, as they may offer fresh perspectives or strategies that can help break through barriers to progress.

Safety Concerns: In situations where there are significant safety risks involved, such as severe trauma or mental health issues, it's essential to prioritize the well-being of the individual. While spiritual support can be valuable, it should not replace professional help from therapists or counselors who are trained to address these specific concerns. Seeking assistance from mental health professionals alongside spiritual support can ensure a holistic approach to addressing the issues while prioritizing the safety and welfare of the individual.

Accountability and Discipleship: Accountability and discipleship play crucial roles in spiritual growth and development. By engaging with a supportive community or mentor, individuals can receive guidance, encouragement, and accountability in their journey of faith. This can involve participating in support groups where experiences are shared and mutual support is provided, or seeking a mentor who can offer personalized guidance and support to deepen one's relationship with God. Such relationships can foster ongoing growth and help individuals navigate challenges more effectively within a supportive community.

Overall, each consideration highlights the importance of recognizing when additional support or guidance is needed and the potential benefits of involving trained professionals, experienced individuals, or supportive communities in addressing various spiritual, emotional, or mental health challenges.

Careful Selection of Support

The process of healing and personal growth often necessitates support from others, but it's imperative to be discerning in selecting the right individuals to assist you along your journey. This selection process should involve careful consideration of whether potential supporters have undergone their own inner work, resolving their own emotional and psychological knots. It's essential that they possess the requisite training and experience to effectively aid others in their healing journey.

Support from someone who hasn't addressed their own unresolved issues can be detrimental rather than helpful. Their unresolved struggles may inadvertently influence the guidance they offer, potentially leading to ineffective or even harmful advice. Therefore, choosing someone who has walked the path of personal healing and possesses the necessary skills is paramount.

Furthermore, it's crucial to recognize that each individual's healing journey is unique, and there's no one-size-fits-all approach. Whether you opt for self-guided healing or seek assistance from others, maintaining patience and remaining open to the guidance of the

Holy Spirit are essential. Committing to the process of untangling the knots of your past requires steadfast dedication and a willingness to confront difficult emotions and memories.

As you navigate this journey, it's important to remember that you're not alone. God's presence and guidance are ever-present, offering comfort and strength along the way. Additionally, drawing upon the timeless wisdom and insights from Christian authors can provide valuable guidance and support.

In conclusion, as you work through your memories and emotions one step at a time, trust in the transformative power of God's healing grace. Embrace vulnerability, remain patient, and believe in the possibility of attaining the freedom and wholeness that you deserve. Each memory untangled brings you closer to realizing your true potential and experiencing profound personal growth.

Conclusion

As we come to the conclusion of "Untangling Knots in Our Past: Navigating Unresolved Memories through Biblical Wisdom" we find ourselves standing at the threshold of profound personal transformation. Throughout this journey, we have traversed the intricate landscapes of memory, trauma, forgiveness, and healing, guided by the timeless wisdom encapsulated in the Scriptures.

In the opening chapters, we embarked on a journey to understand the origins of the knots that entangle our past, recognizing the profound impact of familial spirits, generational influences, and the transformative power of forgiveness in the healing process. We explored the complex nature of memories themselves, acknowledging their ability to shape our perceptions and experiences, whether positive or negative.

As we delved deeper, we uncovered the path to reclaiming our potential, integrating insights from psychological theories with biblical guidance and professional support. We learned the importance of shifting to a strategic and prayerful approach in navigating the complexities of our past.

At the heart of our exploration, we unraveled the knots through memory processing for healing, understanding the roles of voluntary and involuntary memory reflection, and embracing the cleansing power of emotional release. We confronted the effects of trauma on memory, learning strategies to navigate the shadows and emerge into the light of healing.

Moreover, we embarked on the journey of embracing healing and overcoming the weight of self-rejection through insights from Christian authors and biblical inspirations. We discovered the transformative potential of giving and receiving help in the healing process, celebrating progress and growth along the way.

Through personal stories of untangling knots, we found solace and inspiration in the reflections of others, realizing that we are not alone in our struggles. We identified common knots and their manifestations, equipping ourselves with reflective practices to unravel them one by one.

As we reach the conclusion of this transformative odyssey, we are reminded of the importance of patience, vulnerability, and the guidance of the Holy Spirit in our journey towards healing. We recognize that personal growth is cultivated through inner reflection and the protocol of entering into self-deliverance, supported by a careful selection of support systems.

In essence, "Untangling Knots in Our Past" is not merely a book but a roadmap to liberation—a testament to the resilience of the human spirit and the transformative power of biblical wisdom. As we bid farewell to these pages, may we carry forth the lessons learned and the insights gained, embarking on a lifelong journey towards wholeness and healing; guided by the light of divine wisdom.

References

Scriptural References:
1. **Forgiveness and Healing**:
   - Ephesians 4:31-32 - On the power of forgiveness.
   - Matthew 11:28 - Invitation for rest in Christ.
   - Psalm 34:18 and 147:3 - God's nearness to the brokenhearted and healing.
2. **Memory and Self-Reflection**:
   - James 1:22 - Encouragement to apply biblical truths.
   - Philippians 4:8 - Focus on positive thoughts.
   - Psalm 139:23-24 - Prayer for God to search our hearts.
3. **Self-Acceptance and Identity in Christ**:
   - Genesis 1:27 - Being made in God's image.
   - Ephesians 2:10 - Being God's handiwork.
   - Galatians 5:1 - Freedom in Christ.
4. **Emotional Well-being**:
   - Isaiah 43:2 - God's support through trials.
   - Psalm 107:29 - Calming the storm.
   - John 14:27 - Christ's peace.
5. **Practical Faith and Action**:
   - James 1:5 - Wisdom from God.
   - Ecclesiastes 4:9-10 - Strength in companionship.
   - 2 Corinthians 10:5 - Taking every thought captive.
6. **Professional Guidance**:
   - Proverbs 11:14 - Safety in multiple counselors.
   - 1 Thessalonians 5:18 - Gratitude in all circumstances.
   - 2 Corinthians 12:9 - God's power in weakness.

Psychological Theories:
1. **Behaviorism**:
   - B.F. Skinner - Operant conditioning and behavior modification.
   - Ivan Pavlov - Classical conditioning and response to stimuli.
2. **Humanistic Psychology**:
   - Abraham Maslow - Hierarchy of needs and self-actualization.
   - Erik Erikson - Stages of psychosocial development.

Christian Authors:
1. **Frank Hammond** - "Overcoming Rejection": A guide to healing from rejection.
2. **Joyce Meyer** - "Healing the Soul of a Woman": Insights on spiritual resilience.
3. **Neil T. Anderson** - "The Bondage Breaker": Spiritual strategies for overcoming negative thoughts.

4. **Max Lucado** - Quotes on forgiveness and moving forward.
5. **C.S. Lewis** - Insights on the importance of letting go of the past.

Research Studies:
1. **Memory Formation** - Studies on prenatal memory development and the lasting impact of positive memories on well-being.
2. **Trauma Therapy** - Research by Dr. Bessel van der Kolk and Dr. Judith Herman on therapies for trauma like EMDR and the importance of narrative.
3.

Personal Narratives:
1. **Author's Stories** - Personal reflections on past experiences and the process of healing from emotional wounds and self-rejection.
2. **Testimonials** - Stories from individuals who have navigated their own healing journeys.

Practical Resources:
1. **Counseling Services** - Recommendations for seeking professional therapy and counseling.
2. **Support Networks** - List of community and church-based support groups.
3. **Prayer Guides** - Examples of prayers for healing and inviting the Holy Spirit into the healing process.

Author's Note

This book intertwines the richness of Scripture, the depth of psychological wisdom, and the authenticity of personal testimony to offer a pathway to healing. Readers are encouraged to engage at their own pace, seeking the Holy Spirit's counsel and professional guidance as needed. This journey is a testament to the transformative power of faith, self-reflection, and the courage to face one's past.

This reference section serves as a guidepost for readers, providing them with the necessary tools and context to navigate the content of your book and apply its wisdom to their personal experiences.

AttACEs (Adverse Childhood Experiences) is a framework used to assess and measure traumatic experiences during childhood. There are 10 assessment areas or categories in the ACEs questionnaire:

1. **Emotional Abuse**: This category includes experiences of verbal abuse, constant criticism, and emotional manipulation by a parent or caregiver.
2. **Physical Abuse**: This assesses whether an individual experienced physical harm or abuse by a parent or caregiver during childhood.
3. **Sexual Abuse**: This category focuses on any unwanted sexual advances, molestation, or abuse experienced during childhood.
4. **Neglect**: Neglect involves assessing whether an individual's physical and emotional needs were met by parents or caregivers. It includes factors like lack of food, clothing, or emotional support.
5. **Household Dysfunction**: This area explores various types of household dysfunction, including witnessing domestic violence, substance abuse, mental illness, or having a family member incarcerated.
6. **Parental Separation or Divorce**: This assesses whether parents separated or divorced during an individual's childhood.
7. **Mental Illness in the Household**: It measures whether someone in the household had a diagnosed mental illness during childhood.
8. **Substance Abuse in the Household**: This category examines whether a family member had substance abuse issues or addiction problems.
9. **Violence Against the Mother**: It assesses whether an individual witnessed physical abuse or violence directed towards their mother or a female caregiver.
10. **Incarceration of a Household Member**: This area evaluates whether a family member was incarcerated during the individual's childhood.